SERENA,

Thanks 4

Everything!

The Complete Writer

Best,

[signature]

12/2011

Praise for The Complete Writer

The Complete Writer is a well-written and useful guide for beginning and experienced writers of any genre. The authors explain the hows and whys of publishing, from writing the first draft to querying and preparing the manuscript for publishers. From their combined experiences in writing and publishing, the authors know what information to include. They write directly to the reader. Reading this book is like listening to them personally. They really know their stuff. I'd recommend the book as a text for writing classes and seminars as well as a useful tool for any writer. ~ *Ellen Gray Massey*, teacher/adviser of *Bittersweet, The Ozark Quarterly* and editor of *Bittersweet Country, Bittersweet Earth, The Bittersweet Ozarks at a Glance.*

•••••

A unique compilation of advice for writers ... from freelancing and networking to self-publishing and marketing. The book is written by four writers, each with a distinct point of view. If you are serious about creating and marketing your book successfully, this is a 'must buy' addition to your reference library. ~ *Brian Jud*, author of the Publishers Weekly title, <u>Beyond the Bookstore</u>.

•••••

The Complete Writer will cut a novice's learning curve in half. It has everything a new writer needs to turn a passion into a business and dreams of authorship into reality. ~ *Rebecca Forster*, USA Today best-selling author of <u>Hostile Witness, Silent Witness</u>.

•••••

The Complete Writer has much new information and passion about the writing process. This is a promising book and a great product. ~ *Carolyn Howard-Johnson*, author of <u>The Frugal Book Promoter</u>.

•••••

A book filled with readable and practical information for writers. Written by four different authors with diverse backgrounds and viewpoints, it offers valuable advice to any writer. The book covers a broad range of topics from writing and freelancing to self-publishing and marketing. ~ *Dan Poynter*, <u>The Self-Publishing Manual</u>.

The Complete Writer

A Guide To Tapping Your Full Potential

by

Beverly Walton-Porter
Mindy Phillips Lawrence
Pat McGrath Avery
Joyce Faulkner

Red Engine Press
Key West, FL

Published by Red Engine Press

Many of the chapters first appeared as articles on web sites
www.Suite101.com and www.ScribeQuill.com

Library of Congress Control Number: 2005903042

ISBN-10: 0-9745652-6-1
ISBN-13: 978-0-9745652-6-1

Illustrations by Mindy Phillips Lawrence

Printed in the United States of America

Quantity discounts are available on bulk purchases of this book for
educational institutions or social organizations. For information, please
contact the publisher:
Red Engine Press
1107 Key Plaza #158
Key West, FL 33040

Acknowledgments

Special thanks to R J, who means more to me than words could ever describe.

Brittany and Jonathan Porter, for being the best two kids a mom could ever have.

My mother, Shirley Walton-Thayer, who believed in me from the very beginning.

My late father, Leo C. Walton, Sr., for showing me the magic of words.

Beverly Walton-Porter

Thanks to my sons Dan and Grant and daughter-in-law Jennifer.

To the only father I'll ever know and cherish who taught me to look up words in a dictionary instead of using him as a Merriam-Webster and ...

To my wonderful birth mom who helps me in so many ways.

Mindy Phillips Lawrence

Thanks to my husband Everett, my sons Chris and Mark for always believing I can do whatever I want to do.

My mom and dad, I wish I could hand you a copy of this book and be warmed by your smiles.

Pat McGrath Avery

Thanks to my daughter Carmel, my son Nathan and my husband John.

Joyce Faulkner

Introduction

Truth is a complicated concept. Intertwined with perspective, philosophy and emotion, it's almost impossible to take a position on any topic without someone challenging its validity. Authors are a fractious lot. We all think we know best -- and one of the things we know for sure is that the other guy is doing it wrong. Perhaps the only truth about writing is that excellence and mediocrity are equally obvious to the reader. To writers, it can only be found in the beat of our own hearts and the scratching of our pens.

When my partners and I decided to compile this manual, we realized that we are all very different people. We are from separate parts of the country. Our personal philosophies are all over the map. Our educational backgrounds range from Art History to Chemical Engineering. We have worked in schools, state and local governments, small businesses and large corporations. We write fiction, nonfiction and poetry. One of us started a writer's support group. Another runs an e-zine for writers, still another is a publisher. On first glance, the reader might find our work schizophrenic. However, I believe truth is a tapestry of ideas and experience. What we offer the novice writer is the richness of our diverse perspectives. Sample our wares and enjoy.

Joyce Faulkner

The Complete Writer

FREELANCING

The Complete Writer

1

Live Your Freelance Writing Dream!

by Beverly Walton-Porter

Live to write. Write for a living. Think it's only a dream? If so, think again -- because thanks to the endless freelancing writing opportunities on the Internet, your dream of earning a living with your writing can become a reality.

My name is Beverly Walton-Porter and I'm a professional writer. For many years I dreamed of writing for a living and in May 1997, that dream became a reality. Through this chapter, I hope to make your writing dream a reality too.

In this book, I hope to give you the encouragement and motivation you need if you're considering writing for part or all of your income. Some of you may simply want to be published. That is fine, but the reality is that publishing is a business. Editors mean business. Writers should realize that they're expected to treat writing as a business too.

As a full-time freelance writer, I feel obligated to assist novice writers find the information and encouragement they need to meet whatever writing goals they set for themselves because when I was a neophyte, others helped me.

Writing is a journey that never ends. There is no one point where you'll reach the top of the mountain and say, "I know all there is to know about writing."

Before you begin your travels into the realm of freelance writer, I'd like to share five points of light to guide you along your trip. Read them, consider them and mold them to fit your circumstances.

Oh, and one more thing: have a blessed and exciting journey along the written road to publishing success!

Five Tips For Making Your Freelance Writing Dreams Come True

1. **Be Specific** -- First and foremost, you must have a specific vision of how you want to succeed as a freelance writer. Not everyone fits into one mold. Some write for specific niches, such as health or finance publications. Others, such as myself, prefer to diversify and write for a number of publications on a variety of subjects.

2. **Believe In Yourself** -- Believing in yourself and cultivating your own unique brand of creativity is to celebrate and honor the gifts that have been given to you in this lifetime. There is no shame in discovering your true purpose and then following it with gusto and determination. There is only one of you. Gradually work to become more comfortable with yourself and to believe that with a smidgen of confidence and an open heart, you can accomplish any goal you desire.

3. **Network with Other Writers** -- Writing is a solitary profession for the most part. When the time comes to sit down at your computer and bang out an article, essay, short story, novel or poem, it's pretty much you and a blank screen -- and a cup of strong coffee, if you're like me.

    Still, no writer is a success without others. No matter how talented you are or how dynamic your prose might be, along the way I'd be willing to bet you had plenty of support from other people -- and some of the best support you can get is from other writers.

    Networking with other writers adds a dimension of familiarity and a sense of belonging to a larger, like-minded group. Writers understand the terror of rejection. They remember the jubilant rush of the first publication. They know other writers in a way that non-writers cannot.

    Invest in a group of close-knit people who share your vision of writing and who can boost your morale or loan you a crying shoulder when you need it. After you've finished moaning over your latest rejection, they'll help you start submitting work again. When you feel like the publishing industry has shunned your work forever, you'll appreciate the value of these people. Just because writing can be a solitary profession, that doesn't mean it has to be a lonely one.

4. **Be Committed --** Like combing your hair, brushing your teeth or exercising your body, so must you dedicate yourself to writing each day. It's not necessarily the most talented writer who becomes the most published, but the most committed. If you write once or twice a year and submit only on occasion, how can you become a bestselling author? In order to live your ultimate dream, you must focus on your goal, map out small daily steps to make steady progress and work until you reach it -- no matter how many months or years that may take.

So-called "overnight success" takes fifteen years -- or so say experts. Ask yourself what small step you can take today to set yourself on the path toward your goal. What about joining a professional writing group? How about attending a writing conference or workshop? Why not learn how to write a query letter and begin sending one to an editor each week? Commit yourself to action and you've cleared a major hurdle.

5. **Allow Yourself to Fail - And To Succeed --** "Allow yourself to fail?" you repeat in horror. "How can you say it's okay to fail?" Because, fellow writer, it is through the lessons of failure that one learns what it means to succeed. Not every thing you write will be a gem. Much of your work may never be published. What's more, there is nothing wrong with that.

To reach our greatest potential as writers, we must write ... and write ... and write. Repetition is the mother of skill. The more you write, the more you sharpen your talent and expand your abilities.

Don't be afraid to take chances. Some of you may have heard that it's safer to stay with one genre or specialty in writing. There are good points to support that argument. However, one prevailing question remains: if you don't expand your horizons as a writer, how will you ever grow in your abilities?

By the same token, don't be afraid to succeed. It may sound crazy, but many writers are afraid of success. They ask themselves, "What if I succeed and then I can't handle the pressures of success?" It is true that once you reach the stage of what you consider success, you may begin to doubt your abilities. You may feel like a sham. You may feel you've been lucky, but you don't have the mettle to cope with the larger assignments that are coming your way. What to do? Step back. Relax. Refocus. Understand who you are, where you came from and where you are going.

With both failure and success come zingers of all shapes and sizes. Once you know who you are as a writer, it's much easier to anticipate whether it's smarter to dodge energy-sapping obstacles or to confront them head-on.

When you remain focused and committed, believe in yourself, exude passion and have a circle of unbending support around you, the fallacy of failure versus success diminishes. The only thing that matters is your dream of writing and how you choose to live it. Don't be afraid to take the first step today.

first published at *Suite101* (www.suite101.com)

Developing an Effective Press Release

by Beverly Walton-Porter

In the beginning, you may be shy about writing a media release for yourself. Don't worry, that's natural. This isn't a personal thing. It's about business and the product you have to sell which is your writing.

Do other business owners have any compunction about using media releases to announce their company's products, services or events? Of course not. Neither should you, because your writing IS a business.

Traditional train of thought concentrates on the standard media release, which is a facts-only release, but there are a couple other types of releases you'll want to try. Write the release based on the event you're announcing and the market or publication you're sending to.

Most of the time, your media release will be printed verbatim -- unless the editor decides to assign an article out of it. In fact, you may want to write your release like a short article. There's a chance that the editor will print it as he/she receives it.

I once sent a media release to a local newspaper announcing my work's inclusion in an anthology and they chose to assign a reporter to cover a "local woman makes good" type of article. This fortuitous set of circumstances delivers a power-packed punch of publicity (how's that for alliteration?) in that the writer receives free publicity and the book itself may generate sales from the article.

Some releases give just enough information to entice the editor into contacting the writer. Like the media release above, this can often result in a longer article and perhaps an interview.

What goes into the building of a successful media release? You could ask countless Media release pros and gather a laundry list of characteristics, but here are some traits your release should have, at the minimum.

Five Basics Of Building Press Releases

1. Keep the media release short -- my advice is never to go over a page. Editors receive LOTS of releases on a daily basis -- you'll need to catch their eye -- and quickly.

2. Build the media release around the event. You might be relaying "just the facts, ma'am," but that doesn't mean your release has to be bland. Write attention-getting headlines and copy for all your releases.

3. URGE your reader to act on your media release. Get creative and use strong nouns and verbs.

4. Hook your reader in the first two sentences, using the "who, what, where, when, why and how" of journalism.

5. Eschew weak or passive writing in favor of strong and ACTIVE writing. That means getting rid of adjectives, adverbs and ambiguous words. Favor strong verbs and nouns delivered in simple, easy-to-read language.

Anatomy Of A Press Release

FOR IMMEDIATE RELEASE: Place these <<CAPITALIZED>> words in the upper left-hand margin. <<SKIP TWO LINES>>

Contact Information: Provide your name, telephone and fax numbers, both office and home numbers. <<SKIP TWO LINES>>

Headline: In bold type, write an attention-getting headline. Use strong verbs and nouns! <<SKIP TWO LINES>>

Dateline: Put the date you are sending the release, as well as the city you are mailing it from. <<SKIP TWO LINES>>

Lead: Paragraph: Get right down to business and make the first couple sentences of your first paragraph grab the reader by the throat and hold their interest. Employ the journalistic technique known as the five W's and one H -- who, what, when, where, why and how.

Body: Now that you've hooked your reader with the lead, be sure to use the body of your release to expand on the facts you delivered in the first paragraph. Be sure to use strong nouns and verbs and AVOID adjectives and adverbs, if at all possible.

Conclusion: Recap your announcement and highlight any additional information that might boost your release. For freelancers, this might include a sentence such as: "Jane Fabeetz is currently working on her third book [NAME OF BOOK HERE] and is currently booking creative writing workshops for the year 2005. For more information, contact Jane Fabeetz at [PHONE NUMBER} or e-mail Jane at jfabeetz@mailbox.com"

Type these <<CHARACTERS>> at the bottom of the release to signify that the press release has ended.

PRESS RELEASE EXAMPLES: To view sample media releases to get a feel for the rhythm of writing they use, here are some links to media release examples.

http://www.prWeb.com/

http://www.prleap.com/resources/sample_press_release_format.html

http://www.stetson.edu/~rhansen/prguide.html

http://www.free-publicity.com/sample.htm

http://www.Webmastercourse.com/articles/killer-press-release/

http://www.press-release-writing.com/sample-press-release.htm

Are You Ready for Full-Time Freelancing?

by Beverly Walton-Porter

When is the right time to go from a part-time, moonlighting freelancer to a work-at-home full-timer? In this piece we'll discuss how to assess your readiness so that your entry will be as smooth as possible.

I understand there are a lot of you who freelance part-time and maybe you're never planning on going full-time. Hey, that's no biggie. It's not for everyone. However, there are people who want to make the leap, but uncharted waters scares the doodles out of them.

To be sure, making the decision to go full-time is not for the faint of heart. If you're the type of person who has to have a future that's predictable and who has to have everything just "so" all the time, then don't freelance full-time.

What does it take to be a full-time freelancer? There are many combinations of traits and it's true that all freelancers aren't alike but I contend that if you're a full-time freelancer, you're probably an optimistic, confident risk-taker.

Some people may say, "Oh no! That's not me! I'm very well-organized and blah blah blah." I disagree. In your heart of hearts, you are a pioneer. You have chosen to go where most men and women never dream of traveling: into the wild, unpredictable wilderness of working without a net.

It means you are not guaranteed the same paycheck every two weeks like most workers. Your job doesn't guarantee health care or dental insurance -- although you can sign up for such plans through writers' unions. You have to go out and find jobs over and over again. You have to be a marketer, a salesperson and a publicist. You not only have to sell a product, you also have to sell yourself.

By the same token, there are benefits to freelancing full-time, not the least of which is the satisfaction of being your own boss. You can work anytime you want -- day or night. You set your own hours.

However, you must be disciplined enough to work without supervision. You have to motivate yourself each morning to get up and get cracking. Of course, nothing inspires people more than a looming house payment.

What are the telltale signs that you're ready to consider striking out on your own as a full-timer? Here's a list to get you thinking:

- ✔ Increasing sales. Are you pulling in assignments on a consistent basis? Have you gone from selling four articles in one year to selling forty? If so, this is a good indicator of your ability to sustain regular assignments.

- ✔ Have you mastered the art of composing an effective query letter? Are your queries hitting the target more often than not? If so, this is a good indicator of full-time readiness.

- ✔ Are you good at multi-tasking? Can you manage many jobs at once? Writer, administrator, marketer, salesperson, promoter, publicist, researcher and producer?

- ✔ Can you put it together a pleasing product and deliver it on time to your client?

- ✔ Do you have a strategic planner hidden inside? You should know how to think ahead and decide how many assignments you plan to tackle for the next month, six months or a year.

- ✔ Are you good at research? Being able to hit the ground running with interviewing and research, as well as writing on the fly, are assets. You don't have time to be inspired or motivated as a freelancer when deadlines are looming. Motivation and inspiration often equals butt in chair (as I've heard many times before!). One caveat: beware of too much research -- you don't have to be the world's foremost expert on a subject to write a decent article about it. Get the best facts you can and the best, most well informed sources you can. Interview by e-mail when possible -- when you get the experts' replies in their own writing, it's hard for them to say they've been misquoted!

✔ Can you handle interruptions and complete your writing assignments despite all sorts of scenarios that may pop up? Because time means money when your bounty pays the bills.

✔ Finally, do you have a financial Plan B? What I mean is this: until you get the hang of full-time freelancing and are firing on all eight cylinders, do you have a nest egg or a spouse to help pay the bills when they come due? When I began freelancing full-time back in 1997, I made sure my family could live on my husband's salary. It was tight, to be sure, but we met the basics and there were places I scaled down our lifestyle and saved money. Things are more difficult now since he died unexpectedly in 2001. You can never foresee the future, so plan with care!

In no way does this article cover all the ins and outs of making the leap, but this can at least give you a jumping-off point for exploring all the avenues and the pros and cons of your future decision.

first published at *Suite101* (www.suite101.com)

The Professional Pitch: Mastering Query Letters

by Beverly Walton-Porter

How do you interest editors in your ideas, so you can turn them into published pieces? Through a query letter. However, query letters scare the daylights out of many writers. Ever gone on a job interview? Ever written a resume? Ever read a resume? What do all these things have in common with a query letter?

Job interviews, resumes and query letters are all means to sell yourself and what you have to offer. In this case, you are hoping to sell (or pitch) an idea to an editor in hopes of securing an assignment.

In this piece, we will learn how to craft a knock-your-socks-off query letter and break the rules just enough so that you'll get editors and publishers to take that second look at your proposal. When your query letter causes a double-take, then you can bet the chances are good you'll get a go-ahead for the project.

Basic Query Letter Elements

Good news. Each time you send out a query letter, you don't have to reinvent the wheel. All you have to do is refine it a bit to fit your proposed market.

Regardless of what publication you're querying, here are some basic elements you should always include:

- ✔ Current date

- ✔ Your name, address, city/state/zip, telephone number and e-mail address. If possible, use letterhead -- computer-generated letterhead is fine.

- ✔ Editor's name. If you don't know which editor to address, look at the publication's masthead or call their editorial offices and ask a secretary.

- ✔ Correct mailing address of publication

- ✔ Always thank the editor for his/her time and consideration

Your query letter should include a paragraph which explains the article idea you're pitching, why you believe the editor should be interested in the article and why their readers would enjoy such an article.

Briefly explain to the editor how long the proposed article will be and any special points you'd like to highlight. For example, do you plan to interview experts in a given field? Find the fresh angle or element in your proposed article and underscore those points for the editor.

Tell the editor why you can be trusted to write the article. Why are you the writer for this assignment? If you raised Arabian horses all your life, then you have a head start because you have expertise in that area.

Don't assume you have to be an expert on a subject to write about it. I've written about transplant surgeons, storm chasing and professional baseball and I'm not an expert in any of those fields. What I did have was an insatiable curiosity about each of those subjects which led me to seek out fascinating interviews with top-notch experts and to ferret out the most current information available.

If you have publishing credits, don't be afraid to list them. Are you a member of many professional writing organizations or have you won awards? Convince the editor of your professionalism. Don't be afraid to blow your own horn a little.

What if you're a beginning writer and have no credits? Don't worry; everyone starts out with no credits. It's like the old Catch-22 of "how do I get a job when I've never had a job before." As we all know, we eventually DO find that first job and we build from there. It's the same with writing assignments.

If you haven't had any articles published in magazines, think about what else you can mention. How about your church or local club newsletter? Have you had a letter to the editor published? Did you win an essay contest in your local community? If your answer is "yes" to any of these things then mention these in your query letter.

On the other hand, if you have NO writing credits whatsoever, do NOT gush in the query letter: "I am a new writer who has never been published and I would be so very grateful if you would give me a chance to write for you!" Instead, tell the editor you have been writing for X number of years, or you've been pursuing a career in writing and recently joined a local writing group, etc. Maintain professionalism and courtesy at all times.

How Long Should It Be?

The standard is one page for query letters.

Query Letter Example:

Below is an example of an actual query letter I wrote and which landed me an article assignment.

Beverly Walton-Porter
Street address
City/State/Zip
Phone number
E-mail address

CURRENT DATE

Editor Mary Q. Jones
ParentZine
Street address
City/State/Zip

Dear Ms. Jones,

Recently I sent you a query letter expressing interest in writing some articles for *ParentZine*. You responded with an invitation to send ideas.

As a parent, I like to obtain as many fun and creative craft ideas as I can for my kids -- which is one reason why I look forward to each issue of *ParentZine*. In addition, I want tips and information on how to be a more effective parent and spend more quality time with my kids.

As an Internet surfer since 1991, one resource I've discovered that has a wealth of information is the World Wide Web. There are numerous Web sites for parents and children alike. Several more popular Web sites, such as Parent's Place, Manic Moms and Parent Soup also give information and practical advice on common parenting questions.

I believe your readers would enjoy an article which lists and reviews Web sites strictly for parents and children. Each web site listed would have a brief description of what each site offers, as well as highlights of must see info found there.

There are numerous resource sites available and with an estimated 250 million people connected to the Internet by the year 2000, I believe this would be a timely issue to address. Instead of spending time using Internet search engines to find the best resource sites for parents and kids, I can do the work for your readers.

This article could be a one-time piece between 600 to 1,000 words, or a series of shorter pieces tailored to the needs of the season (i.e. Great summer getaways for families with their corresponding WWW sites for more information).

My previous writing credits include published articles and essays in *Writer s Digest, Show & Tell Magazine, Domestique Magazine, What's Love?* and *The Colorado Springs Sun,* among others. Currently, I write monthly computer software review articles for CompuNotes and a bi-weekly column for *@WRITERS* electronic magazine.

One of my how-to articles, "Eight Great Ways to Jump-start Your Writing," is posted on the Purefiction Web site (www.purefiction.com) and was chosen Best of the Net by The Mining Company Web site (www.miningco.com).

Professionally, I am a member of the Oklahoma Writers Federation, Inc., Romance Writers of America, Sisters of the Scribe and am serving my second term as President of the Enid Writers' Club, the oldest organized writing group in the state of Oklahoma. I also self-publish *Scribe & Quill,* a monthly newsletter for writers.

Again, thank you for considering my ideas and I hope to hear from you at your earliest convenience. Meanwhile, if you should need a freelance writer for a specific assignment, please don't hesitate to contact me at the above-listed phone number. I would be glad to tackle any article assignment on spec and tailor it to your needs.

Sincerely,

Beverly Walton-Porter

This query letter landed me a 500-word assignment for which I was paid $450. That's almost a dollar per word, which is a decent take for any writer, in my estimation.

Another Example:

The query letter below landed me a go-ahead for an article, but you'll notice I did something slightly different in this query -- I attached my writer's bio/resume instead of listing my credits in the letter itself. This is an option you may want to use when you've built up enough publication credits.

Beverly Walton-Porter
Street address
City/State/Zip
Phone number
E-mail address

CURRENT DATE

Ms. Bonnie Brenton
Today's Oklahoma
P.O. Box 12345
Oklahoma City, OK 73152-9971

Dear Ms. Brenton,

Recently, construction was completed on the largest music recording studio in Northwest Oklahoma. Now owner/professional musician Jerry Champagne is one step closer to reaching his goal of producing slick, chart-topping records from this area of the state.

Jerry, who has thirty years in the music business, opened Champagne studios in September 1991 with an eight-track analogue recorder and a few outboard processors. Since then, the studio has grown into its current status as a fully automated twenty-four track recording facility.

The studio measures two thousand square feet and offers the perfect equipment and setting for musicians and vocalists to translate their talents into commercial successes. Jerry and his staff offer additional perks, such as mobile recording and in-house single CD demos.

His studio played an important part in Oklahoma history when Julie Black-Davis selected Champagne to help produce her Labor of Love Project for the Oklahoma City bombing victims. Proceeds from the sale of Julie's cassette, "The Stars that Lite the Sky," benefited the Feed the Children Foundation and sold thousands of copies.

Would you be interested in this story for Today's Oklahoma? The article runs 1,000 - 1,500 words and focuses on Champagne Studios and how its expansion and modernization signify big things for Oklahoma in the field of music and hit recordings.

Lively and fast-paced, the article introduces readers to another interesting person, place and project happening within Oklahoma. I can offer the feature written to your specifications and delivered on deadline. Color photographs are available, as well.

With the addition of Champagne Studios' larger recording studio in Northwest Oklahoma, our area of the state will gain more publicity and a chance to showcase more of the natural talent we have here in the state.

Your readers would find the story especially interesting since Oklahoma has strong connections in the music field with Garth Brooks, Reba McEntire, Brooks and Dunn and other country stars who have Oklahoma roots. Champagne Studios could become a future link to Nashville, as well as other music meccas and Oklahomans need to know about it. Through your magazine, they will.

Attached you'll find a list of my qualifications and publication history. For your convenience, I have enclosed a self-addressed, stamped envelope for your reply.

Warmest regards,

Beverly Walton-Porter

As you can see, each of these query letters addresses a different topic and article, yet each has common elements. Now you can see what I mean by not having to reinvent the wheel each time you write a query letter. All that's needed is some tweaking to fit the current subject you're pitching!

General Housekeeping

Keep your query letter a clean, mean business machine. Looks count, so avoid the following:

- ✗ Bright-colored paper, perfumed/artsy paper, handwritten queries, queries with stickers on them and other such cutesy expressions. Save them for your friends, not editors. Always use white or buff-colored paper, preferably twenty pounds or more. I prefer twenty-four pound paper with computer-generated letterhead.

- ✗ Spelling and grammar errors. If you mean "their," don't write "there" instead. Mind your commas, periods and semi-colons. If you're not sure how to use colons or semi-colons, **don't** use them at all.

Send clips of your work IF you have them, although an editor can get some idea of your writing ability and style from your query letter, adding clips of your previous work can boost your pitch.

Don't forget the SASE!

Some writing and freelancing rules can be bent or broken IF you know what you're doing and why. Not much is written in stone, but there is one courtesy you should always observe when you're sending out query letters -- ALWAYS ENCLOSE A SELF-ADDRESSED, STAMPED ENVELOPE (SASE).

If you send your query letter through snail mail and you neglect to enclose an SASE, you run the risk of never hearing anything back in response to your query. Editors and publishers are not going to pay postage to respond to the hundreds of query letters they receive on a yearly basis.

Be Patient with Editors!

Editors have many job duties in addition to slogging through query letters and full submissions. Please respect and understand how busy editors are. As one who has been on both sides of the fence, I can attest to this fact. When I worked as a review editor for *Eye on the Web*, I had one hundred, eighty Web site reviewers working for me. At the time of *EOW*'s demise, I had no less than fifteen hundred Web site reviews outstanding, meaning they were submitted and ready for me to edit and then send for posting on the site. The reviewers who were courteous and didn't inquire fifty million times a day about their Web site reviews were the ones who tended to receive more assignments. This sounds harsh, but in the publishing world, it's reality. As I've mentioned before, the publishing business is just that -- a business.

How Long Should I Wait?

In general, expect to wait eight weeks for a response. I've found that queries sent via e-mail usually receive faster responses.

If you haven't received a response after eight weeks, send a courteous follow-up letter. Resist the urge to call the editor.

After your follow-up letter, wait two more weeks. If you haven't received a response, then you may want to call the editor and leave a message. Editors are approachable, but make sure you aren't going overboard. The last thing you want to do is come off as a nuisance.

From Ether To Editor: How E-Queries Make Your Life Easier

by Beverly Walton-Porter

Electronic queries, or e-queries, are becoming more and more common. What are e-queries, you ask? Quite simply, they are nothing more than query letters which are sent through e-mail as opposed to regular mail, or "snail" mail.

E-queries can make life SO much easier for writers when it comes to selling articles. Many editors prefer e-queries, although there is still a die-hard group of editors who require regular mail queries. I predict that most, if not all, editors will move to e-queries.

For *Scribe & Quill*, I prefer e-queries. I also prefer submissions through e-mail rather than regular mail. Things seem to go much more smoothly on all counts.

It's easy to pop into my mailbox, read a query letter and respond. Best of all, the writer doesn't have to wait for days for the postal service to deliver. In a matter of seconds after I hit "send," he or she will receive an answer. If there are questions, a follow-up message can be sent back in a matter of minutes. Smooth, fast and NO stamps or envelopes required.

When you compose an e-query, you should make it as professional as one you write on real paper. Just because e-mail seems informal to many people, you shouldn't treat it casually. In this case, it's a business tool. In fact, most of my queries are sent through e-mail these days.

All the elements of a query letter sent through standard mail should also be present in your e-query. The format should remain the same. Make sure to include your mailing address and telephone number on your e-query. An editor may want to contact you by standard mail or by phone.

In an e-query, type directly into an e-mail message rather than add it as an attachment. Some publications may request attachments, but if they don't, write it up as a regular e-mail message. As for *Scribe &*

Quill, it states in our guidelines that we don't accept e-mail attachments for queries or submissions yet every week I still receive attachments. How do I handle those? I e-mail the writer and tell them attachments aren't accepted and to please resend pasted in regular e-mail. I'm a lot nicer than some editors who would trash the submission and not take the time to reply. Why? Because it may seem like ONE small reply, but if you receive twenty of those weekly, after ten weeks, that's two hundred e-mails!

As a precaution and for record-keeping, I would recommend that anything you send to an editor through e-mail, you send as a copy to yourself using the CC (carbon copy) line in your e-mail program to mail a copy to yourself. This goes not only for e-queries, but for articles you submit. Although e-mail is a reliable means of communication, I have had a couple of articles that were never received by editors when I sent them and had my own copy to prove it.

Although some people are reticent about using technology to its fullest extent because they clamor for a true, hard copy of their submissions, I recommend that you try at least one e-mail query. There is no good reason to shun e-mail as a tool for procuring more writing assignments.

You have to slog through a lot of frogs to find a prince and sometimes you have to slog through a lot of queries before landing a gem of an assignment. Make it easier on yourself by using all the tools available to you.

E-queries cut down on turnaround time. Granted, you can't make an editor answer you faster through e-mail, but you'll know the same day an editor gives you the "yes" or "no" -- and you won't have to wait three to seven more days for postal handling. Those three to seven days gained will allow you to get to work reworking your query and resending to other markets.

If you're convinced and ready to test the waters with an e-query, here is a short checklist to follow before hitting the "send" button:

✔ No fancy fonts or unique e-mail stationery. Just because you can do wonderful backgrounds with some e-mail software, that doesn't mean this is the time to use them. Follow the same rule for snail mail queries. Don't make it fancy, just neat and professional. In an e-query, a white background and black type (ten- or twelve-point, Times New Roman or Sans Serif (Arial) font will suffice.

✔ Electronic queries do not give one a license to be informal. This is still a professional letter to an editor, so "Hiya there, Bob!" won't cut it. Use all your salutations and closings as you would a query sent through regular mail.

✔ Always send a copy to yourself. I recommend saving a copy on a disk labeled "my queries" or printing them out and placing in a file folder.

✔ Add your mailing address and your telephone number to all electronic query letters. You never know when an editor will be inclined to pick up the phone and CALL you about an assignment. It's happened to me!

✔ Type your e-query directly into an e-mail message. Do not send as an attachment unless it has been requested by an editor. The trouble with attachments is that not everyone uses the same word processing software and why go to the trouble of guessing when you can just type it right in the e-mail message? Simpler is better.

✔ Use your spell check before hitting the "send" button. Make final checks for grammar and punctuation errors.

Once sent, begin another query. See how easy it is?

first published at *Suite101* (www.suite101.com)

Quick Clips: Writing Book Reviews

by Beverly Walton-Porter

What is one way to collect published clips of your work and get you started on your way? Why, book reviews of course!

Anatomy of a Book Review

What's the secret to writing a successful book review? You must try to strike an equal balance between describing the book's general content to readers and offering an objective, unbiased evaluation of the book itself.

As with any other type of writing, be sure to consider your audience when writing a book review. Will the literary crowd, the mainstream crowd or romance crowd read your review? Knowing the answer to this question is important, because you must communicate to these readers in a certain way.

There are many elements that are integral to the process of writing a review. Obviously, you'll need to read the book and as you read, be aware to keep your focus on these things and take notes:

- ✔ Look over the table of contents (if the book is nonfiction). How is the book organized? Are the chapters well organized and in logical order according to content?

- ✔ For fiction books, know the genre of the book and be familiar with other books in this genre so you can contrast and compare. If you're writing for science fiction fans, you should know the reader audience and be acquainted with other science fiction novels.

- ✔ Who authored the book and what other books have they written? If reviewing a nonfiction book, how is the author an authority on the subject?

- ✔ How does the author relate to readers of the book and from what point of view? Is the book's style formal or informal?

- ✔ If you're reading a fiction novel, be sure to focus on theme, plot, setting, characterization and point of view. What worked, what didn't and why?

- ✔ If you're reading a nonfiction book, ask yourself if the information provided to readers is accurate. Check other books in the field, if possible.

- ✔ Determine if the book succeeds in accomplishing what it set out to do. For instance, if you read a horror novel, did it scare the wits out of you? Were the characters more than cardboard cutouts? Was the plot unlike any other you have read in this genre?

Going to Great Lengths

The length of a book review is determined by the requirements of the publication. In some cases, my book reviews are only three hundred words long. In other cases, the book review can stretch to twice that many words. Check with the appropriate book review editor and be sure to follow writer's guidelines to the letter.

Heading Things Up - The Right Way

When you are ready to put your pen to paper and write your review, make sure to include the following important information at the top of your review, for example:

Title	<u>Beyond the Boundary</u>
Author's name	Jane Fabeetz
Publisher's name	Red Engine Press
Publication date	April 2005
Number of pages	252

24

ISBN number	978-09512354-9-9
Price	$6.99 paperback/$2.95 e-book

Study Other Book Reviews

Still not sure you have the hang of it? Here are some sites that publish book reviews. Take a look at the offerings at these sites and use them as a guideline for the techniques you will incorporate into your writing.

ALA's Booklist	http://www.ala.org/ala/booklist/booklist.htm
Amazon	http://www.amazon.com
Barnes & Noble	http://www.bn.com
BookPage	http://www.bookpage.com
BookReview	http://www.bookreview.com
BookSpot	http://www.bookspot.com
Bookwire	http://www.bookwire.com/bookwire
L.A. Times Book Reviews	http://www.calendarlive.com/books/?track=mainnav-books
Midwest Book Review	http://www.midwestbookreview.com/
The New York Review of Books	http://www.nybooks.com/
New York Times Book Reviews	http://www.nytimes.com/pages/books/
Salon Magazine's Sneak Peeks	http://salon.com/books/index.html

This is by no means a comprehensive or complete list, but by reading the material posted at these sites, it will give you a better idea of how book reviews are written.

Beyond the Book Review

Don't stop with books, because in this world of technology, there's much more to review -- computer software or hardware, for instance.

When you head out on your search and query mission, make sure you leave all avenues open. Search for sites that publish reviews of any kind and ask if they have an opening for a reviewer. Many times you'll find a steady assignment that way.

Each hardware or software review publication has its own formatting rules. Be sure to follow them. Be familiar with the tone of the publication.

first published at *Suite101* (www.suite101.com)

Rejection Redux: How To Turn a Negative Into a Positive!

by Beverly Walton-Porter

Every writer faces rejection. The question is how you will choose to face it and turn the negative into a positive. Fail to deal with rejection and you'll find yourself facing writer's block. Not only that, you'll be feeding into fear -- a freelance writer's worst enemy.

In this chapter, I will teach you how to use the energy of rejection to fuel you toward more assignments. Feeling sorry for yourself or beating yourself up with self- criticism does no good. In fact, it hinders your writing and is a detriment to progress.

After examining rejection and the various reactions to it, you will learn how to take a PRO-active stance, rather than a RE-active stance when you open up the mailbox and get a generic form letter that usually says, "This doesn't meet our needs."

Rejection is not the end for any writer. It is actually a wonderful beginning and an invitation. Sound crazy? You might think so -- but let me assure you, it's even crazier when a writer allows rejection to hamper efforts to gain more acceptances or sales. Remake your rejections into acceptances -- I'll show you how.

Not All Rejections Are The Same!

Believe it or not, not all rejections are created equal. "What?" you scream. "Isn't a rejection a rejection?"

Well, yes and no.

There are different levels of rejection. The level of personalization you receive in a rejection letter can act as an indicator of how close you are coming to acceptance of your work and ultimately, publication and/or payment for your words.

The first level of rejection is the generic form rejection. Typically, it reads like this:

Dear Writer,

Thank you for submitting your work to our publication. Unfortunately, your work does not meet our needs at this time. However, we thank you for your submission and wish you the best.

Sincerely,

I. M. An Editor

If you've received this type of rejection note from a major magazine, chances are you and hundreds of others received the same exact note.

Here is the reality of the publishing business: editors are generally overworked and underpaid. They READ a lot. They receive a LOT of material to read. Imagine coming to work every day and facing mounds upon mounds of manuscripts for consideration. It's up to you to slog through all the mess to find that ONE literary pearl. It can be daunting, it can be tiresome, it can be overwhelming, to say the least.

Now, how can you have the TIME and ENERGY to respond to each of those submissions personally? The answer is, you can't. Not if you plan to come back tomorrow and receive MORE manuscripts from the postal carrier or in your e-mail box and begin reading them while completing your other editorial duties for the upcoming issue.

What To Do About This Type Of Rejection:

Keep resubmitting to this publication, each time playing a game with yourself to see how close you can get to a more personal reply. Go over your submissions or query letters with a fine-tooth comb. See what you can do to hone in more specifically to what the editors want. Read an issue or two of the publication and analyze it. Strive for a more personal response or an acceptance the next time around. Vow to eventually crack this nut.

This brings us to the second level of rejection: the form letter with a personal, handwritten message or adhesive note attached. When an editor takes time to WRITE a personal note or scrawl a message on an adhesive note and sends it to you, this means that you made some kind of impression that warranted the editor taking EXTRA time out of the day to send you a more personalized reply.

What To Do About This Type Of Rejection:

Take this as a positive sign and begin drumming up a new query to send to this editor and do this as quickly as you can. When you send your new query, make sure you mention that you were delighted with the note and that you're pitching another idea that you believe will appeal to the readership of the publication. Get something else in the mail RIGHT AWAY. This is a case where you need to "strike while the iron is hot"!

The third level of rejection is the personal handwritten or typed letter from an editor. Not a form letter, but a personal letter that talks about specific points in your manuscript or query. Editors, in general, don't take the time or energy to do this unless they're REALLY interested in the writer's potential.

What To Do About This Type Of Rejection:

Stop what you're doing and begin working on another submission to this editor. This is your chance to impress the editor with your prompt response and to demonstrate your willingness to rework material or resubmit material that will fit the publication, based on the personal letter you've received.

When you send off your submission, be sure to include a gracious, personal note to thank the editor for taking the time to reply. Mention that you've taken the suggestions or comments under consideration and have reworked your piece accordingly, or that you're querying a different article idea altogether. The main point it to acknowledge appreciation of the extra time taken to respond to your work in such a personal way.

Finally, the next step is not a pure rejection -- it's an acceptance of the general idea of your query but with a twist. Here's an example (one that happened to me). I queried *Writer's Digest* with an idea for an article. The assistant editor liked the general idea, but wanted a different take on it than what I'd presented in my query letter. She wanted to know if I'd be willing to write the article using the slant she'd provided -- and oh, by the way, if I could get it done by so-and-so date, then they'd publish the piece and pay me $100 for it. Needless to say, I jumped at the opportunity.

Was this a rejection? Yes and no. Let's call it a partial rejection. The original idea was not what the editor was looking for, but she would publish an article IF it was written to her specifications, using her slant. This illustrates vividly WHY you should never write an article in full BEFORE querying first. Why waste time writing 1,500 words of an article that won't ever sell? Spend time crafting the best query you can, then write an article once you get the go ahead.

Yes, there are different levels of rejection letters. Pay attention to all of them. When you're first beginning your writing career, it's possible that you'll receive a LOT of "level one" rejections. After a while, if you continue to write diligently and on a daily basis, you'll begin to see your rejections take on a more personal flavor. This is a clue that you're writing is becoming sharper, your queries are becoming stronger and you're getting closer to publishing success.

Why You Should Never Take Rejection Personally

Rejection. OUCH! What a painful word. No one likes rejection. When you're a writer, it seems so much more personal and hits right in the heart and soul of your being. "How can I NOT take rejection personally?" you ask.

Emotions are important. The trick is to USE those emotions in a constructive way. The editor who rejected you will probably never meet you in real life. You're a name on a sheet of paper -- out of hundreds, perhaps thousands, of names. Sad, but true. Use the emotions you experience from your rejection to spur you on to work THAT much harder on your next submission to a different editor. Be PROactive, rather than REactive. Turn that negative into a positive, driving force.

Editors don't like to send rejections; they love to accept good writing. It makes their lives easier. So don't take the editor's reaction to your work personally. You're not a clueless, talentless idiot. The piece just isn't right for the editor and that's that. Another editor might love your piece and buy it. Editors are humans and they are subjective in their judgment. I like cats better than dogs. I prefer a cat story to a dog story -- it's all subjective. It doesn't mean the dog story is a bad story -- just means that I prefer cat stories. A simple example, but true.

If you write, you will get a rejection at some time in your life. Face it and then consider the ways you'll use those emotions to motivate yourself to improve your writing and to find a way to get published. Again, Richard Bach: "A professional is an amateur who didn't quit."

I'm an emotional person. I cry at soppy movies and I cry over tragic world events. When it comes to rejections, I've grown a thicker skin and I've learned how to use the emotion from rejection letters to motivate myself to succeed -- somehow, some way. I've gone from ZERO publication credits to about two hundred. If I'd allowed those rejections to rob me of my heart and spirit, I never would have realized the JOY of seeing my words in print. I never would have realized the JOY of writing full-time. I never would have realized the JOY of writing these course chapters to help YOU succeed in your writing dreams.

Next time you receive a rejection, remember one of my favorite sayings: "They can get the silverware out, but they CAN'T eat you." Sometimes it gets mighty scary when you hear those editors sharpening those blades, getting ready to slice you up as a writer - getting ready to blast you verbally. Ignore it. Smile, if it kills you. Plot your next course of action. Use that rush of emotion to whip out five more queries that same day. Redirect that emotional rush, instead of reacting negatively to it.

If all else fails, e-mail me and I'll be happy to engage in a little "writer's rejection therapy" with you. Why? Because I believe you can go as far as you want -- YOU hold the key -- they DON'T.

Rejected! Now What?!

The day has come. The dreaded moment is upon you. You've read the letter. Now what do you do? First of all, you heed the above advice and manage your emotions, using them as fuel to begin your next project or to embark on your next plan of action. Before you do that, you must do one more thing: you must design and use what I call a "post-rejection checklist." Why bother with this? Simple. It'll help you analyze any trouble spots you need to smooth over before you launch into your next phase of action.

Once you've gone through the checklist listed below, you will have

31

answered any lingering questions and you will know what glitches need to be worked out in the process of preparing your next query or story submission. Be honest and fight to maintain an objective view of your work. It's difficult to gain the distance you may need, but it's essential to do so.

Post-Rejection Checklist

After reading your rejection letter, ask yourself these questions. Answer them honestly:

- ✔ Did I follow this magazine's SPECIFIC guidelines regarding word count, manuscript format and style of writing? In other words, make sure you didn't do the obvious faux-pas -- like sending a romantic fiction story to a magazine that doesn't accept ANY fiction.

- ✔ Did I check my manuscript for spelling or grammar errors?

- ✔ Was my manuscript typewritten and sent in the accepted (or requested) standard format (i.e. typewritten, double-spaced with ample margins on all sides?), or through e-mail, as a requested WORD attachment or pasted directly in e-mail as the guidelines stated?
  - If my query idea was rejected, was my letter only one page long?
  - Did it include all the elements of a successful query letter?
  - Was I too vague in my proposed article pitch?

Figure out, to the best you can, what you can improve upon before you slip that same manuscript or query letter BACK in the mail and into another editor's hands. By asking the RIGHT questions and revealing the RIGHT answers, you can increase the odds of getting a "yes" next time, instead of a "no".

MARKETING

The Complete Writer

Capturing Local and Regional Markets

by Beverly Walton-Porter

In this chapter, we'll discuss how to use local and regional media sources for free publicity. In order to reach your most effective level of marketing and publicity as a freelancer, you'll need to adopt what I call a three-pronged approach to getting your name and your services out there:

✔ Local/regional marketing/PR

✔ National/global marketing/PR

✔ Internet/electronic marketing/PR

Many of you might be ashamed or embarrassed by "selling yourself," but what you need to do is shift your perception so you realize that this is not a personal thing -- it's a business situation. You are like any other business -- you ARE a business, in fact.

Although you'll be shooting for a global approach for your freelance business, be sure not to neglect the local or regional markets for your business. Envision tendrils reaching out from your local/regional area, growing and reaching a wider audience from there, expanding from there into different states and countries. Then envision those tendrils reaching into the electronic media -- the Internet. This will be the final way you will put your three-pronged approach into action.

Before you can tackle the world -- both the mundane and the digital, you must begin in your backyard. You could be overlooking some of the most lucrative projects that exist right where you live: in your own town, county, state or region.

Making a List - Checking It Twice

Whether you live in a small town or a big city, before you can unleash a full-fledge marketing/PR attack, you need to draw up a method to your madness. In other words, you need to brainstorm and make up a list of potential contacts. You can either write this up in notebooks (the old-fashioned way) or you can make a folder in your computer in which to keep this contact info.

You might also want to set up a database (highly recommended) to track your contacts and the dates and outcomes of each. The key is to come up with a SIMPLE, workable system for knowing who you've contacted and when. Don't spend an exorbitant amount of time on this. It's important, but don't make this task an excuse to keep you from accomplishing more important things, like writing and querying.

Not sure where to begin your list? Try people you may know already as building blocks for your burgeoning local or regional PR/marketing foundation:

✔ Relatives

✔ Friends

✔ Ex-coworkers

✔ Business acquaintances

✔ Organizational contacts

✔ Church members

✔ Neighbors

✔ PTA or caregiver contacts

For each of these contacts, consider what type of business or organizational contacts these people have and how they might be willing to help you expand your horizons.

Some communities offer free advice to small-business owners as provided by retired executives or managers. Check your local phone directory for groups that might be of assistance to you.

Ten Ways to Kick Your PR Machine into Motion

1. Begin with a media release to local and regional newspapers. Most newspapers have a local business announcement section and this section trumpets promotions, new businesses and transitions within the business community. This is where you need to send your Media release. Your release will be short and sweet and will inform members of the community that you have launched "XYZ Freelancing and Consultation Services".

2. Send your Media kit to ten targeted businesses or organizations. Include your Media release, a bio, copies of sample published pieces, your business card and any other materials to support your kit.

3. Call up any business or organization contacts you already have and make an appointment to visit with them and tell them in person about your new business and the services you offer. Sometimes it's all in who you know. Ask them for referrals.

4. Make up low-cost brochures and ask local businesses if you can leave some in waiting rooms or on community boards. Temporary agencies will occasionally allow you to do this. I had one temp agency that stopped doing resumes and they would give out my card to anyone who walked in and requested a resume. It was good business for them and for me.

5. Distribute business cards freely! When you make a contact, whether personal or professional, give that person your card.

6. Get with the local library and offer to present a free seminar on a Saturday afternoon. At the seminar, distribute all your PR materials with samples in packets for attendees. People love free seminars and they are often inclined to contact you for paying work afterwards.

7. Contact schools in your area. Visit with the principal or teachers and explain the writing and editing expertise you have. Suggest a student writing contest and offer to judge it for them. When the contest is written up in the local paper (via your media release, of course!) you'll get PR AND your name

out there as a business in the community.

8. If you don't have a writing group in your area, develop one. If you have a writing group in your area that is generic, specialize. Do you write business-related articles? Found a local group of business writers. What better way to bring recognition and prestige to your efforts?

9. Contact your local community college or Vo-tech and send them a proposal for you to teach a course on writing -- whatever your specialty is. Be sure to include your Media kit along with a list of references and contacts. Many Vo-techs are open to summer courses on writing. If you're hired as an instructor, you'll not only get paid for your efforts, you'll be sure to get PR at no cost to you through the school.

10. Does your community have a local cable-access television station? If so, more often than not you can produce your own television show on writing for free. Don't worry about freaking out in front of the television. Visualize yourself talking to a close friend in place of the camera and you'll ACE the moment. Invite local guests and members of your writing group so you won't have to go solo. Get DOUBLE PR for FREE.

Smart Marketing: Slanting Articles for Print and Web Publications

by Beverly Walton-Porter

I hope you've discovered the usefulness of the idea generation technique and you've been working on mastering those query letters, because the smart writer sends out query letters FIRST, instead of writing an article that might not sell "as is."

In this chapter, I'll be discussing several things:

✔ **How to target the proper markets**

✔ **How to avoid the ONE MISTAKE most all new writers make!**

✔ **How to "mine for gold" to dig up potential article sales markets**

✔ **How to employ a "Q & A" technique to zero in on a potential market**

✔ **What rights you should offer - and should you sell "all rights"?**

✔ **Important things you should know about writing for the Web versus writing for print pubs**

✔ **Suggested places to search out traditional print media markets**

Now What Do You Do?

Now that you have an idea and you've polished it down to a gem that reeks saleability, what then? Answer: target your markets and increase your chances of selling the finished product to both print and on line publications.

As I've said before, being a writer is more than being a writer -- especially when you are a freelancer. The second hat you'll wear is one of marketing professional. Thanks to the Internet, marketing your work via e-mail and by Web syndication is a boon and a blessing to writers.

If you fail to wear the hat of savvy, smart marketer, then it's like having a great steak and trying to sell it to the neighborhood vegetarian. No matter what you say, your client won't be in the market for meat, period.

In this piece, you will discover how to find places to pitch your work. You'll also find out the best way to succeed and one guaranteed way to fail. The goal is to avoid the latter and become skilled at the former. Take these bits of wisdom and then apply them to both print and on line markets.

Mining for Gold

Finding writing markets is a lot like mining for gold. Some of the time you come up with prospects, or little hints of gold-colored flakes of fool's gold and occasionally you'll hit a jackpot of opportunity.

There are four elements to successful writing market searches: usage of Writer's Market, subscriptions to writer's magazines, weekly searches on the Internet's writing databases and Web sites and finally, setting up a networking arrangement with a group of like-minded freelance writers.

When these four elements work together, you'll have constant exposure to writing markets for fiction, nonfiction and poetry. You can plan on setting a certain amount of time aside each week for market research. This time is not wasted. It mines the way for your future publishing success. Be sure you concentrate on conducting your research for traditional print media, as well as on line venues.

Writer's Market, an annual publication by Writer's Digest Books (now published on CD ROM, too), is a reliable standby for thousands of writer's guideline listings. Whether you write books, essays, poems, gags, short stories, scripts or more, Writer's Market is sure to point you to some great resources.

However, Writer's Market should be the starting place for your search. You should also subscribe to writing magazines such as *The*

Writer, *Writer's Digest* or *ByLine* for current updates on the writer's marketplace.

Writer's Digest, my favorite magazine for writers, publishes fifty to sixty market listings in each monthly issue. Once a year, they'll publish a list of the top markets for writers. These used to be mostly print publications, but now you can find a mixture of markets.

The third element of successful marketing strategy consists of weekly visits to writer's guideline databases found on the Internet. You'll also need to bookmark any writing sites you visit which feature new or emerging market information.

You'll need to keep an eye out for brand a new writing site cropping up on the 'net. From these sites, select only the ones that offer the most current and relevant information as it pertains to you and then stop by those sites every week.

Finally, I can't say enough about networking with other writers. Most writers are generous when it comes to sharing possible markets for article or story sales. If you're not already involved with an on line writing group, embark on a serious search to find and join one.

The ideal group will lend support and encouragement, will be open and expansive to new writers and will keep flaming and undue criticism or cynicism to a minimum.

Last, but not least, your group should share new writer's markets and guideline information on a regular basis. The goal should be to assist all members in attaining publication success.

Once you know where and how to locate writing markets, the next step is to target your proposed article. Ask any editor about mistakes most writers make when querying their publication and most will mention "writers who send inappropriate material for our magazine."

What does that mean? It means sending a children's story to a women's confession magazine; it means mailing a short story to a magazine that only publishes essays or nonfiction articles; it means mailing poems to a short story publication.

Before you commit this major faux pas, learn to analyze and understand how your proposed article will fit with the markets you're researching.

Using the Q & A Method for Smart Targeting

Just as we used the question/answer method for identifying and understanding our reader audience for possible writing projects, we can use the same question/answer method to further refine and target our publication markets.

Take another look at the article idea you've chosen to market. Ask yourself these questions:

- ✔ What publications are interested in this subject matter? Are they a traditional or on line publication?

- ✔ Who are their readers -- and what other similar or related publications might they read?

- ✔ When is the best time to query this article idea? For instance, if you plan to write a holiday-related article for a magazine, the lead time is generally six months prior to the holiday you're writing about. If your article addresses the Christmas season, don't expect to send in a query in late November and expect your article to make it in December's issue.

- ✔ Where are your target markets published? Are those magazines based in New York City, Los Angeles, Montana or overseas? Take into account the tone of the publication and make sure your tone matches theirs. For instance, writing for Manhattan-based fashion magazine calls for a certain style or tone to the articles they publish. If you're planning on pitching your article to this sleek, uptown rag, you'd better sure your article comes off just as sleek and sophisticated.

- ✔ Why should the editor be interested in your article? Be truthful. Be objective. What are you going to deliver in your article that will persuade him or her to buy it for the magazine's select group of readers?

- ✔ How will you approach this publication's editor? Does the

41

editor accept e-mail queries? If you're not sure -- ask, don't assume. Again, consider style and tone of the publication. In general, on line venues need writing that's short and to the point. No one wants to read page after page on the Web crafted in long, boring paragraphs.

Okay, you've learned to run your article idea and editor approach through the Q & A mill again. Now what? It's time for a heart-to-heart chat about ...

Working Smarter

The sooner you learn how to work smarter and faster as a professional writer, you'll find more sales will come your way.

Whatever you do, be sure you don't make the one mistake ninety-nine percent of new or intermediate writers make when they try to sell their articles to magazines or on line pubs. What is this one mistake? Writing the article in full before sending a query letter to see if the editor is interested in the subject of your article. Paste this near your computer: DO NOT WRITE AN ARTICLE WITHOUT QUERYING THE EDITOR FIRST. "I have to write this article ... I KNOW it'll sell!" you whine. Are you sure? How do you know? Only editors wield the power of acceptance or rejection in their hot little hands. Unfortunately, you must produce the work these editors are searching for, or you'll earn one of those horrible form letter rejections. You know, the kind that reads: "Sorry. Your work doesn't meet our needs at this time." What? Don't try to figure it out; the message is clear: thanks, but NO thanks.

What the editor wants is what the editor will accept for publication, or purchase from you. Regardless of how much you're in love with this splendid article of yours, the basic truth is that it may never sell.

Now, it's possible you have written complete articles for the purpose of having samples of your writing on hand for an editor. This is okay and does not relate to the point I'm trying to make here. It is fine to work on pieces for your writing portfolio, but don't make a habit of spending undue amounts of time and effort pounding out articles for magazines without querying those magazine editors first.

What Rights Should You Offer?

One thing you need to learn about before you think about sending out your work is the issue of publication rights. Although some people would rather believe otherwise, writing is always a business from the publisher's point of view.

You may not care for the business end -- perhaps your goal is just to have something published, period. If you're a novice, often your insatiable quest for publication can cause you to overlook crucial aspects which are designed to help protect you and your work.

Do yourself a favor: don't gloss over the importance of learning the basic business of writing. At the very least, you must learn about the main categories of publication rights, how they are defined and most important, how they relate to you and any work you produce.

We will not tackle foreign rights, syndication rights or rights dealing with screenplays, motion pictures and other like material right now. Here I will offer brief descriptions of the rights most commonly offered by publishers and extended by freelance writers. Should you wish to delve into the subject further, you might consult more comprehensive works strictly dedicated to the subject, or purchase the latest edition of *Writer's Market*, published yearly by Writer's Digest Books. Contact information is provided at the end of this chapter for your convenience.

First Serial Rights or First North American Serial Rights:

When a writer sells first serial rights, or First North American Serial Rights (abbreviated as FNASR), the newspaper or magazine is granted rights to first-time publication of your work. You retain all other rights and may resell them accordingly.

Simultaneous or One-time Rights:

The right is given to publish the work on a one-time basis. These rights are NOT exclusive. So you may sell your work to other publications at the same time.

For the writer, this is a good position to be in, from a business standpoint. Whenever possible, you should try to put yourself in a position where you can sell a story or article to more than one market at the same time.

Admittedly, publications do not care for this arrangement because they want to have exclusive rights to your work.

Second Serial or Reprint Rights:

The publication has the right to print an article or other piece of work which has already been printed somewhere else. Exclusive rights are not granted in this case. You, as the author, have the freedom to resell your work.

Because of the nature of the business of writing, the more reprints a writer can get out of a story or article, the better. Not only will you receive more publication credits to add to your writing resume, you'll also enjoy getting paid more than once for the same article.

An analogy I often use is the soft drink. Think of the most popular soft drink in the world today. Now, is each can of this soft drink produced in a way so it tastes different? Of course not. It is the same product and yet the company sells the product to more than one market.

Would it benefit the company to sell one can of their product to a single person or organization? Of course not. To earn the most profit, the company sells their unique product to consumers, vendors, retailers and wholesalers.

By the same token, if you have a unique article which has proved successful with readers in the past, why would you want to sell it only once and limit your earning potential (and your publishing potential)?

With the right marketing savvy you can resell that same article to a handful of markets or more.

All Rights:

If you should agree to sell all rights, you will never be able to use that work again. Once sold, the written piece is no longer yours.

Many writers are dead-set against selling all rights because of this all-encompassing agreement to cut all ties to one's work. Deciding to sell "all rights" is a choice based on the length of the article or story, effort involved, payment offered and prestige of the publication.

For instance, a close friend of mine sold all rights to an article and based her decision, partly, on the prestige of the magazine involved. She knew she would gain recognition and coverage from having her work in this publication that it would not only afford her more name recognition as a high-profile writer, but it could also lead to better and more high-paying assignments by association.

One Important Reminder:

You should also know that unless you and the publisher agree otherwise in writing, the Copyright Law of 1978 states you are selling one-time rights. Unless specified otherwise, that is what you're offering to the publisher.

Electronic Publishing - Where Does It Fit In?

Electronic publishing on the Internet can be a boon to writers. Because of the opening up of electronic markets, writers now have more opportunity to see their work displayed in e-zines and on Web-zines. The Web has had a tremendous impact on freelancers and publishers around the globe. These days, writers have the opportunity to sell to countless on line Web-zines -- some pay, while some do not. Most of my work is sold via the Internet. My query letters and articles or stories are sent via e-mail to the editor and I cannot remember the last time I fashioned an actual paper query letter.

Along with the wide-open new world of writing opportunities on the Web, there comes a whole new set of issues for writers and publishers to face. One of the hot issues deals with electronic rights. When a writer publishes on the Web, what rights are you selling? Often, it's hard to tell. Rule of thumb: always discuss the issue of rights with the editor. Get it confirmed!

Some Web-zines insist on all rights while others agree to one-time rights. I've also sold reprint rights to e-zines over the Web.

It can be a mess. Posting an article on the 'Net can be construed by some publishers as first-time publication and they'll offer payment for reprint rights only. Be careful. Some print magazines purchase your article and then assume they also have the right to put it in their Web-zine for no additional payment.

The Association of Journalists and Authors (ASJA) and National Writers Union (NWU) are working to secure the rightful payments for writers in this regard. For more details, visit http://www.nwu.org/ or http://www.asja.org/.

Also, just because you land an assignment for an on line venue, don't be afraid to ask for a contract sent through e-mail. In fact, I would recommend asking for a contract. If you don't protect yourself, then you are leaving yourself open for disappointment.

Along with the contract, make sure you keep all e-mail messages you receive from the editor. Keep paper copies of these in a standard file or save on computer disk.

Three Important Things About Writing For The Web

1. Get to the point

2. Keep paragraphs shorter

3. Write "tight," using an active voice   (Example: The dog was walked by John. [PASSIVE VOICE] ~ John walked the dog. [ACTIVE VOICE])

In general, when you are writing for a Web-based publication, you should keep your work to the point and easy to read. If your work is posted on a Web-zine, 'net surfers want a good article or story and they want to get to the "meat" of the work -- and FAST.

The Web is a visual medium and people want quick gratification. If you're writing fiction, avoid long, narrative stories that take several pages to get started. Give readers plenty of character-driven action and make action happen on the FIRST page so readers will "click" to the next page.

On the Web, paragraphs are shorter and there's plenty of white space. Make sure your copy is tight and that each word lends something to the work. Get rid of filler words. Watch for overuse of "that," "just" and adverbs. Use stronger nouns and verbs, whenever possible. Be precise and use direct, concrete words to relate to your readers. Avoid abstract, wish-washy words. Use links to other Web sites or pages whenever possible.

Many 'zines are sent out through e-mail and the same rule applies here. Give your readers good information and plenty of meat to sink their teeth into. A good rule of thumb for e-zines and Web-zines or any Web content is to KNOW YOUR AUDIENCE. Before querying an article to a Web site or 'zine, take the time to subscribe to that 'zine and READ what's been published before. This advice applies to print AND on line pubs.

Articles vs. Essays vs. Fiction

Here's the exception to the "query first, write later" rule: short stories, essays and poetry. The reasoning is obvious when you're talking fiction vs. nonfiction writing. If you're writing nonfiction, you can propose how you'll cover your topic in a query letter. On the other hand, there's no way you can explain how you'll write a poem or short story until you've written it. Send them to the appropriate publication addressed to the correct editor along with a cover letter. It shows you respect the editor's time and consideration AND it gives you a chance to tell a bit about yourself. positive plug NEVER hurts.

How about novels, you ask? Yes, you send a query and a synopsis or chapter-by-chapter outline before sending an entire manuscript. Publisher's guidelines vary, so ALWAYS follow their preferences first. However, you'd better have the manuscript finished, because if the editor is hooked by your query and synopsis, chances are he or she will request the entire book. Be prepared.

Now it's time to put you to work finding markets for your writing. Scared? It's always scary. You never get over that apprehensive feeling. But at the same time, the whole event is exhilarating. Just think: YOU are doing something that most people never do -- you are molding your dreams into reality and ACTING on it.

Don't you feel MAH-velous? You should. I'm very, very proud of you. You've only just begun!

Diversifying Efforts for More Sales

by Beverly Walton-Porter

So you might be asking yourself, "What's next?" What's next is the professional freelancer's most valuable strategy -- diversification. Now, some of you may have heard that specialization in ONE area is most effective, but to be truthful, I haven't found that to be the case.

For most professional freelancers I know (the ones who do it for a living, not as a hobby), diversification lends itself to getting more of your work out there. This variety of presentation helps you market yourself into areas that may have been closed to you before.

Diversify ... what?

Just what do I mean by diversification? A sampling of the work I've done in the past will provide an example of the types of writing work I've had assigned, accepted and/or published:

- ✔ numerous articles for a new site devoted to people new to the United States

- ✔ media releases for a company that specializes in Web positioning and e-commerce

- ✔ site content for a distance learning company focusing on global perspective

- ✔ reviews

- ✔ romance trivia

- ✔ book recommendation column

- ✔ interview articles

- ✔ essay/personal experience

- ✔ parenting articles

- ✔ book-length manuscript editing

- ✔ seminar handouts

- ✔ complaint letters

- ✔ resumes

- ✔ cover letters

- ✔ job interview how-to

- ✔ career profiles <over thirty total>

- ✔ professional Q & A articles with motivational speakers, CEOs and authors

- ✔ six-step program for launching an e-zine

- ✔ motivational column for writers

- ✔ article on glutamine for health 'zine/site

- ✔ Web site design and content development

... and the list could get longer. I think by now you see what I mean. There is NO specialization in this list. The key here is diversification. In simple terms, use your talents for all their worth and don't be afraid to step out of your comfort zone and write anything/everything.

How to Diversify - And Why

How do you diversify? How do you know which paths to take?

One way to find out your diversification potential is to take an inventory of your life experience and education. Write down people, places, things, situations or experiences you have been exposed to in your life -- as much as you can within fifteen minutes, maximum. Now, you won't be able to cover everything, but you will cover a LOT of ground. This is akin to free association, so don't allow your internal censor to have a say during this personal/life inventory.

Okay, are you finished now? Great. What'd you come up with? Probably a whole lot.

Now, how do you build a diversification profile from this? Take all the keywords or phrases you wrote regarding your life inventory and then "branch" off of those with types of writing jobs or assignments/articles you could reasonably research and complete.

In other words, let's say you have two children -- you're a mother or a father, right? That alone qualifies you for parenting articles or children's short stories, rebuses or short, Mini Page-type pieces. See what I mean?

Like to read? Love the computer? You can apply your writing talents to write reviews -- books or software, in fact. Many places don't pay for book reviews although you get the book for free and that can build you quite a library. However, many sites are beginning to dole out some sort of monetary compensation for reviews. Newspapers will run freelance pieces and some, like one newspaper in Texas, will pay a pretty good sum.

In short, if you intend to earn money with your writing, you must use EVERY resource and experience you have to write for a myriad of markets. You must diversify and expand your repertoire of written projects. As you do so, you'll discover what's called the "snowball effect." What that means is that where you once had an occasional assignment that paid, you'll pick up one or two more...then MORE. You may get to the point where editors see something you've written and they e-mail YOU to ask if you'd like to contribute an article. Seem far-fetched? Not at all. This has happened to me MANY times.

Why Not Specialize?

Some freelancers would argue that specialization, rather than diversification of assignments, is the way to go. I cannot speak for them; I can only speak for myself when I say that IN MY OPINION, when you specialize in ONE type of writing, you're limiting your opportunities. If you would like to try specializing because you're not comfortable branching out, give it a try.

As you gain experience and clips, you may want to reconsider. Frankly, I don't know who was the first person to tell other writers to write in one genre or form and told them to master ONLY that form, but whoever it was, I can say that their advice never washed for me. Thank goodness I was brave enough to "break" this particular rule. If I hadn't, I doubt I'd be making a living at freelancing.

Write What You Know... And That's It?

Once upon a time, I was preparing to write about a legal issue and happened upon an acquaintance of mine who was a paralegal in another department of the local government building where I worked.

I asked her if I could interview her regarding this subject. She stopped, looked at me like I had ten heads and with a patronizing, dismissive glance replied: "I think you should follow that advice about writing what you KNOW about. If you don't know anything about the subject, you shouldn't try to write about it."

At that time I was a new writer and my ego was very fragile. She made me feel like a puppy that had been spanked. "Who was I to write about anything?" I wondered. Then, as the year tagged along, the more I thought about it, the angrier I became. I decided that I could write and I would write about anything I pleased -- I would show her that I was up to the challenge.

Now, with nearly two hundred published pieces under my belt, my first book contract AND my own well known literary agent, I'm so thankful I didn't allow her to snuff out my creative drive and desire. An excellent lesson that illustrates that some advice is just not worth taking -- in fact, some advice is worth going against.

What does this anecdote have to do with you?

Well ... you've heard the sage advice, "Write what you know," haven't you? In the beginning, that's an oft-used counsel to get novices started on their journey. However, I can tell you that as you progress and mature as a writer, you'll begin writing articles about unfamiliar topics. Think it's impossible? Think again. In the past year or so I've written over thirty career profiles and none of these interviews or articles requiring intense research had anything to do with freelance writing.

Here is a sample of the kinds of subjects my editor threw at me -- at two-week deadlines for articles and supplemental articles numbering three thousand words or more:

- ✔ Surgeon, both Thoracic and Transplant

- ✔ Storm chasing

- ✔ Professional baseball -- men AND women.

- ✔ Arborist

- ✔ Systems architect

- ✔ Tailoring clothes

- ✔ Professional bodybuilding

- ✔ Doula and child birthing

- ✔ Osteopathy

- ✔ Biotechnology and technicians

... and once again, the list goes on and on.

I'm not an expert in any of the above -- yet, I was able to research, interview and write my way to over thirty articles in a variety of fields with success and payment for EVERY single one.

What happened to the paralegal who once told me that I should "write about what I'm familiar with"? Well, she's still in her same job years later, still satisfied with not taking any chances. I suppose some people are happy with that, but we writers...well, I guess we have a curious streak and we're determined to succeed on our OWN terms and not on others'.

WRITING FOR BUSINESSES

Making $$$ In the Nonfiction Market

by Pat McGrath Avery

It may not sound as exciting as writing the great novel, but it can pay the bills and allow you to eat well. There are many books out there on making a living as a nonfiction writer. Most of them give detailed advice on the available markets. Check them out.

If you consider yourself a fiction writer, you've probably written nonfiction somewhere along the way. Maybe you reported on ball games and club activities for your high school newsletter. Or maybe you covered famous lecturers visiting your college campus. After school, you may have covered social events or community activities in your local newspaper. In your job, you may have written department manuals, technical guidelines and product promotional materials.

All of these things are nonfiction writing. It is a market with a huge breadth and depth of categories and thus, opportunities. Someone has to write every newspaper article, technical manual, advertising blurb and marketing brochure, so why not cash in on this market?

Go to the bookstore and check out the new book section. There is a high percentage of nonfiction books: biographical, motivational, leadership, management, historical, sports history and the list goes on.

The key to nonfiction is finding a need and filling it. Sometimes, the need is defined for you. A company hires freelancers to write ad copy or department manuals and provides the guidelines. When writing a technical manual for the newest version of MP3 players, you have to know the product and understand the technical level of your audience.

Let's look at some of the opportunities in the nonfiction world:

Newspapers and Magazines

In either of these, you can start in the local markets. Make contact with your local papers. Offer to cover an event for them. Write book or movie reviews and submit them. Depending on the size of your paper, the editor may be searching for fresh writers. Contact her and get to know her if possible. If nothing else, submit for the op-ed page.

Local and regional magazines are the same. Look around and you will find your town has local history and interesting people. I live in the Ozark Mountains of Missouri and our local magazines are filled with stories of people with interesting hobbies, lifestyles and jobs. You may find an older person who remembers when your town was growing, had a new industry, was the home of a famous person or something of interest. Visit schools and find a young person who dreams of the Olympics or wants to be the first doctor in his family.

Communities love human interest stories and people enjoy finding out about interesting people in their town. Most of us live our lives without knowing much of what has happened, or is happening, outside our own backyards. Once you get a story published, others will begin to come to you. Many people have a story to tell or knows someone who knows someone. Keep your eyes and ears open and you will find plenty of material.

Business Writing

There is a world of opportunity here, especially with small businesses. A large corporation will have most of its manuals and internal communications written in-house. Most likely, marketing and advertising has already been outsourced to a professional firm.

However, the small business needs the same materials and very likely does not have anyone in-house with the necessary expertise. What kind of writing might a small business require? Business plans, department manuals, technical manuals, product instructions, letters to customers, marketing and advertising materials -- take your pick.

If you wish to pursue this kind of writing, create your own brochure listing your areas of expertise. Learn about the company that you want to approach. Get to know their product line, the approximate number of employees and who their customers are. Then write a letter to the CEO, enclose your brochure and ask for an appointment with him.

To work with a company, you must meet deadlines and you will have to write for approval. You may be working with an individual or a committee (I much prefer an individual). You will write and that person (or committee) will review and most likely want edits. You will be working back and forth until the project is completed. You are usually not paid until then. Once you have successfully completed a project for a company, it will be easier for you to contract more work. The more you understand the company culture, the product and the employees, the easier it will be for you to represent them.

Technical Writing

Much more detailed knowledge is required for technical writing. You have to understand what you are writing about. If you are writing a technical manual, you have to know how the product works. Then the challenge is to describe it to an audience who does not know anything about it. If you have ever bought furniture or toys to be assembled, you know what I'm talking about. How many times have you had problems following the directions? Sometimes they just do not seem to make sense. Therein lies the challenge -- to make sense of something the reader knows nothing about.

Companies hire freelance writers for this type of writing. You will have to check out each company before you solicit work.

How-to Books

This category allows you more freedom of choice, but you have to know the market to be successful. If you can find a need, one where there is not already a plethora of books on the subject, then research the subject and write about it.

I attended a seminar by Dan Poynter, a leader in the self-publishing field. I had read his books on the subject and knew that he had written in other fields. He told stories about his books and why he wrote them. In each case he found a need and filled it. For example, he had a cat that was getting older and he wanted advice about it. He could not find any books or materials to help him, so through his own experience, he wrote about aging cats. His book was successful because there was nothing else out there.

Even if there are other books on your general subject of interest, look for a special niche. Maybe no one has covered it from a special point of reference. If you find that to be the case, do it. Look at all the business books on the market. How many ways can you talk about leadership and management strategies? The books continue to be big sellers because the author has a unique point of view about the subject.

Corporate managers look for books on leadership, quality and team work. New ideas and new approaches are welcomed. Companies are faced with the constant challenge of keeping market share in a competitive and changing world. To do that, they need to be aware of the latest trends, buzz words and information on management. Success stories are popular. You can see that in the number of CEO biographies where companies were led to new growth.

Motivational Books

Since we all need motivation today and we will need it tomorrow, the motivational field is always open to creative thinking and proven strategies. The field ranges from daily motivational thoughts to full-length books. There are numerous web sites and e-newsletters filled with stories and ideas to inspire us. These range from a religious orientation to general human principles.

There are always calls for stories for anthologies such as Chicken Soup, Cup of Comfort and other series of books. If you have a story to tell, check your writer's newsletters and web sites and look for the open markets. Then submit your story.

Try putting motivational thoughts on your web site. You will need to change them frequently if you have many visitors. Start a blog or journal based on your motivational ideas. Write articles. Make presentations to groups and organizations. Motivational speakers and writers brand themselves. The more recognizable their name, the more likely they are to sell books.

Biographies and History

I am lumping together a huge market. Both fields require research -- lots of it. Both must be factual. Although we know that every writer approaches a subject from his own point of reference, all should try to present the facts as accurately as possible. There is a lot written that is more opinion than fact. If you want credibility in the field, you must be accurate and as unbiased as possible.

Presumably, unless you are trying to make money with an exposé, you will write a biography about someone you admire or have an interest in. You will be trying to paint an honest picture of that person. It will be colored by your perception, your writing skill and the amount of your research. All writing is.

I hesitate to say you can never do enough research. At some point you have to quit studying and start writing. You do need exhaustive research to find sources that tell the complete story from as many viewpoints as possible. If you are writing about history, you will find your research differs based on the timing of the writings. John F. Kennedy's assassination is an example of this. If you read early works and then later works, you will find the emotions of the time colored the writer's vision in the early years. This is true of books about wars. Look at the general attitudes about the Vietnam War from the 1960's to today. After almost forty years, we are recognizing that we never gave the veterans the respect they deserved. We have gone from a nation who criticized them to a nation who appreciates their sacrifices.

Just think about the changes in attitude since the Civil War, in both the North and the South. So if your research covers a time span, look at it through various decades or centuries. History does not change, but our perceptions do.

The General Market

I have only touched on a few of the opportunities available in the nonfiction market. Whole books have been written on the subject -- but hopefully, I have given you some things to think about. There is a world of opportunities out there. Most of us can find a number of topics that interest us. Any research we do for nonfiction can later be used for writing fiction. There are a lot of crossover possibilities.

Keep your eyes open and try the nonfiction market. If you can get started in it, it pays well. It is much easier to sell a nonfiction article than a short story. So give it a try.

Tips for Writing Resumes and Letters for Companies

by Pat McGrath Avery

If you want to write for a living, there are various opportunities in the business world. Writing resumes is one option. It's a certain style of writing and requires the writer to be precise. Each word is important and must carry its weight. A resume is nothing like a novel or a short story. Its success depends on its ability to pinpoint a person's background, achievements and strengths in the fewest words possible. That being said, there are many positives about this type of writing.

There is always demand. Job searches are a constant. Whether the country or an industry is in good times or bad, people will be changing jobs. Every person looking for a job needs a resume. Some people write their own, but most understand the need for an experienced writer with an objective viewpoint.

Numerous firms fill this need. They range from headhunters to career counselors to job search firms -- a rose by any other name is still a rose. These firms prepare resumes and then, depending on their service, offer other job search support.

This is where you, the writer, come into the picture. These firms need writers. Some hire in-house staff, some contract writers and some use freelancers. In many cases, the writer is well paid. However, to get the money, you need to be associated with a for-profit company rather than a government entity. For example, a state program that provides $30 resumes isn't going to pay well, but a company that charges $500 per resume will. Investigate the companies on line, check out their charges, then query them about their writing staff.

Like all business writing, you need to work at securing a company's business. The first step in the resume business is to study the resumes that are successful today. Visit the bookstore or the library and read about job searches. You will find a wide variety of advice, but you need to be familiar with the concepts. One of the most famous job search books, <u>What Color is Your Parachute?</u> by Richard Boles, has

59

been a benchmark for resumes for years. On the other hand, companies that distribute unsolicited resumes will advocate a different style of document.

There are commonalities. All experts advise that resumes must be:

- ✔ Error free
- ✔ Readable
- ✔ Concise
- ✔ Factual

Since it is generally accepted that a resume has about five seconds to capture the reader's attention, it is imperative that it showcase the person and his achievements and strengths in as few words as possible.

There are three major types of resumes: functional, chronological or a combination of the two. Each has strengths and weaknesses. A functional resume is one that highlights achievements and skills by category. It will use key words that are important to the person's industry, skills and position. The chronological resume lists the person's experience by company, in chronological order, from the latest position to the first. Industry usually accepts a combination of the two as the best type of resume. Give some highlights at the top to capture attention and then list the experience chronologically in the bottom to show job history.

Likewise, there are one-page and multi-page resumes. Purpose determines the appropriate length. If the person is following up on a networking contact and she has been asked to submit a resume, then the detail provided in a two-page resume is fine. If on the other hand, she is mailing a resume unsolicited, she needs a one-page resume that will capture immediate attention.

As a writer, the firm will tell you what type of resume to write. You need to be cognizant of what the marketplace will accept, but if you write for a company, you will have little choice in the style. You will be challenged to be creative and paint a strong picture of a person in very few words -- to be factual yet interesting. A resume is nothing more than a marketing tool for a person looking for a job. The level of the person, his experience and the position he wants, will be major determinants in how you format his resume.

Let's take a look at each of the four points mentioned above:

Error-free

Mistakes in a resume are as deadly as bullets. If a resume is filled with misspelled words, poor grammar or misused punctuation, the reader assumes a lack of communication skills, apathy or just plain laziness. None of those attributes are of interest to any company. The circular file is littered with reams of poorly written resumes.

An error-free document takes the job searcher through the first hoop of the process. As the writer, it's your duty to edit and re-edit until the document is perfect. After years of writing resumes, I can't tell you how many times I've forgotten a period or reversed a number.

Most job search firms have an editing staff to do the final review and proofreading. If you strike out on your own, it's imperative that you have an editor. A resume with errors will stop a job search cold.

Readable

It seems obvious that a resume must be readable, but what does that mean? Keep in mind that the document has about five seconds to capture attention. In that time frame, the reader has to identify something special about this particular candidate. From his viewpoint, this person must fill a need or have something unique to offer the company.

How do you, the writer, make sure this happens? What are the characteristics of a readable resume?

- ✔ Short bullets or paragraphs -- remember the outline -- culling information down to the least words possible is your goal. Research confirms that people will not read paragraphs at first glance. Use bullets -- one line if possible. If you need a paragraph, never let it exceed three lines.

61

✔ White space -- the eye needs a break -- a rest from too much print. Look at the document aesthetically. Is it appealing? What catches your eye? Is there enough white space that everything doesn't run together on the page?

✔ Use special effects sparingly. It's acceptable and necessary to use some bold, italics and or underlining in a document. Keep them to a minimum for maximum impact. Figure out what's most important for the reader to see and use the effects accordingly. You will use underlining or italics for book and magazine titles, article titles, etc. Titles never require the use of both. Pick one and be consistent throughout the document. If a person has published a couple of books and several trade journal articles, you will differentiate between publication titles and article titles -- for example, you may put article name in quotes and publication title underlined.

Concise

If you're old enough to remember when diagramming and outlining were part of the English curriculum, you will know what it's like to write resumes. You are outlining a person's life. Remember those reading comprehension exercises where you had to find the theme of a paragraph. That's what you'll be doing. In most cases, you will sift through pages of information, listen to lots of detail in an interview, take copious notes, consider the position and industry of the client and shrink it all down to a concise document that is readable, attractive and strong. Other times, you'll feel like you're writing fiction -- some clients seem to recall next to nothing about their past jobs.

Factual

You are not writing fiction. You have to take facts, use them creatively and present an honest picture of the person, however hard that may be. You will learn to cover people being fired, ex-convicts, people with unaccounted time lapses and those entering the work force after years of being a stay-at-home mom or dad. You will find people who are honest, conservative, outright liars and those with the gift of blarney. As much as writing, you will learn to read people and write accordingly. It's a great way to study human nature. It's also a lesson about the business world, from Fortune 500 companies to the self-employed. You will cover all industries, all sizes of companies and all types of positions. You will also find the educational market requires a different type of document, known as a CV (curriculum vitae), that is extremely detailed. You will find that in trying to prepare a research, technical or professional person for a job search, you may want several documents: a resume, publication or research addendum, testimonials and/or references. There are multiple variations that you will learn along the way.

With the resumes, you will write cover letters. Here is a chance to be more creative. Again, brief is better. However, the object of the letter is to get the reader to look further and peruse the resume. All this is done to get a phone call or an e-mail. Then another facet of a job search takes over and the resume has accomplished its purpose.

Creative thinking and salesmanship are great assets to have for cover letters or any kind of business letters. You need to pack the most punch with the fewest words possible. Always remember that people won't read long paragraphs, crowded letters, or anything that is not pleasing to the eye. That will become your mantra -- brief, readable and original. Not an easy assignment for a writer.

If you pursue this type of writing, you will eventually write follow-up letters, biographies, letters for advancement and all other types of letters related to career choices.

If all this sounds good to you, check out the companies. It's competitive and not always easy to find an opportunity. If you're a good marketer, you might consider soliciting resume work on your own. You'll have competition, but you will be able to write a resume cheaper than a large company will. That's the advantage. The disadvantage -- you have to brand yourself, provide references and be able to sell your service.

Jane Fabeetz

1440 Lakeshore Drive Kansas City, MO 64099

H: 882.719.0123   C: 884.764.2345   jfabeetz@aloa.com

Professional with variety of experiences in office management, Internet/web site, telemarketing and social services.

Assistant to CEO of $10 million company, responsible for support of his sales activities.

Prepare computer analysis on FoxPro, graphic work on Paint Shop Pro.

Built web sites and set up Internet service for clients; provided training.

Diverse experience in running an office including HR, financial, technology, operations and customer service. Computer experience includes: MS Word/Works, MS Office 2000 and XP, MS Front Page, Coffee Cup; can write HTML. Learning Adobe Acrobat, WordPerfect, MS Power Point and Photo Shop.

Education & Credentials

BA, Education, Drury College, Springfield, MO, 1995.. *Academic Dean's List.*

AA, Johnson County Community College, Overland Park, KS, 1993. *Academic Dean's List.*

Licenses: CNA, CSSD, CAD, Johnson County Community College, Overland Park, KS, 1984, 1995, 1996, respectively.

Professional Experience - Business

Sales Coordinator, Renner Corporation, Kansas City, MO, 2003 – Present

Manage client relations through complete process from sales to completion of services; one-on-one client interaction.

Perform various office duties including scheduling, phone and record keeping.

Office Manager, Cass County Gazette, Raymore, MO, 2000 – 2001

General office duties, typed classifieds, layout and proofread paper.

Internet Technician, Inet Solutions, Kansas City, MO, 2000

Client services set up. Handled customer technical queries.

Telemarketer, Dyson Creative Services, Lenexa, KS, 1999

Placed calls and completed orders via computer system.

Professional Experience – Social Services

Social Service Director, Beverly Health Care, Harrisonville, MO, 2002 - 2003

Managed care plans, scheduled doctors, general resident services.

Social Service Director, Friendship Rehabilitation Center, Lawrence, KS, 1993 - 1994

Conducted one-on-one interviews with residents, managed admissions, care plans and doctor visits.

Day Care Provider/Owner, Pike Day Care, Pittsburg, MO, 1988 - 1993

Owned and operated a licensed day care center.

Writing Exercises for Resumes and Letters

by Pat McGrath Avery

Now that we've discussed resumes in detail, we are going to practice. Look through the sample resume for Jane Fabeetz. She has had a varied career and a number of jobs. Because they are so sharply divided by industry, I have separated her chronological experience into two sections: one for business and one for social services. In most cases, you can use a straight chronological listing. The most important things for you to notice:

✔ The listing of her experience in the lead line. This replaces the common idea of an objective. An employer is more interested in your experience than he is in your objective.

✔ The bullets at the top show Jane's major achievements and strengths. Their purpose is to capture the reader's attention.

✔ Listing of her education, credentials and experience in a readable format.

✔ Plenty of white space to make the document pleasing to the eye.

✔ Brevity -- saying things in the least and strongest words possible.

Now we are going to look at another client named Bob. Imagine he sent in the following information and wants his resume written. In reality, I almost always do a phone interview with a client to flush out more detailed information about their successes.

I am the manager of a chain of auto parts store in Lincoln, NE. I've been here for six years but the company isn't doing well financially and I think I need to look elsewhere. The company grew the first three years I was employed. It went from four to six stores around the city.

65

Store revenue remained about the same, but with the additional stores, the total revenue went from $6 million to $9 million. Unfortunately, in the last two years, it has declined and this year's sales are projected at only $7 million total. I'm not sure how to cover that in my resume. I've had responsibility for the operations, but the company quit the local marketing when a new CEO took over.

I have an associate's degree from Cleveland Community College and have taken numerous courses about the industry and management techniques. I've also taken computer courses and was part of getting all stores set up on line. We now do our purchasing, inventory control, payroll information, sales and other functions on line. This saved the company quite a bit of money.

Before that, I worked for three years as an Assistant Service Manager for a Firestone location in Houston, TX. I did quite well there and won an award for customer service. That was my first job out of college.

I attended college on an athletic scholarship. I did make the Dean's List in my last semester.

I'm hoping to find a job that will allow me to grow in my management experience. In my current job, I manage six store managers and through them, about sixty-five people. I don't have to stay in the auto parts business. In fact, I would like to move into a company whose products are more technical.

How do we take that information and make Bob stand out in a crowd?

Let's start with what he wants to do. We know he wants to advance into a better management position. Industry doesn't seem to be important to him, so we don't want to make too many references to the auto parts business. What skills are required to manage people -- what responsibilities does he have? He didn't specifically tell us that he's responsible for sales and profit, but most managers have at least some responsibility for both of those. For this exercise, we are going to assume he does. In reality, it would be one of the questions we would ask him. Typically, managers are responsible for customer service, the operation of the business, the supervision of employees including hiring and firing, purchasing product, managing the inventory, order fulfillment, etc.

So I'm going to start his resume with a sentence that highlights these skills.

"Experienced manager with track record in general management, operations, purchasing, inventory control and customer service."

Now, let's look at what he's done while in his job. He had to play an important role in opening and operating those new stores, so he was partly responsible for the company's growth. I'm going to capture attention right away by listing this achievement. What can we quantify to get attention?

"Key role in company's growth from four to six locations and from $6 million to $9 million annual sales."

He told us he helped save quite a bit of money when they automated operational functions. Another question: how much is 'quite a bit?' Let's suppose we ask him and he says $55,000 per year. That's another accomplishment. That $55,000 is now profit instead of expense. Let's make another bullet:

"Instrumental in saving $55,000 per year by automating operational functions."

Since Bob has a college degree, we want to mention it. We would indicate if he had attended without getting the degree, but the degree is always better. It indicates that he stuck to and achieved, his goals.

"AS, Cleveland Community College." (We will ask him for the year).

"Numerous courses in management and industry training."

This only touches on a few of the concepts of resume writing, but it will give you the opportunity to practice picking out important facts and wording them in a concise manner.

The 'Editing With Clients' Experience

by Pat McGrath Avery

If you're a published writer, you're familiar with editors. Whether they are magazine or book editors, work for a publishing house or are freelancers, we get to know them well. We become a team. They are our friends in the industry and can make the difference in whether or not we are successful.

If you work in the nonfiction world, you also have editors. However, they are of a different breed. They are the owners or employees of the company you write for -- and sometimes they don't seem like our friends. Teamwork isn't necessarily part of the equation. The upside is that if we please them, we get more work. The downside is that sometimes they lower the quality of our work -- at least in our eyes.

When you secure a writing assignment from a company, you will be told the purpose and general style wanted. Then you use your creativity and writing skills to create the document. This is true of any kind of business document from letters to brochures.

Once you complete the document and send it in for approval, it can be easy or very frustrating. Hopefully someone hired you because he appreciated your ability and understood that you are a skilled writer. Usually in this case, a few editorial changes may be made. Often this is nothing more than a correction or clarification of information. This process is relatively short and painless.

However, there are two types of clients who can turn it into a very frustrating experience. One is the committee. If you write for a committee, be prepared to have varying responses to your work. You will likely have as many opinions as there are people on the committee. If the committee functions well, they will have their ideas together and the editing becomes a simple process. If, however, the committee does not function well, then you can be in for a long process. In such cases, they might ask for so many changes that the original document loses its flavor. As writers, we give our best effort to the project. If we find it revised almost beyond recognition, then we dislike having our name associated with it.

The other client who can create a problem for the writer is the one who thinks he is an accomplished writer, too. If he is also a micro-manager, you will wonder why he's paying you to do the work. He will often change the document far beyond your comfort level. He may nit-pick at it until he drives you crazy.

I'm telling you these things not to discourage you, but so you will be prepared and understand that it happens to everyone. I write a lot of resumes for executives and managers. I find this is the field where I most often run into the micro-manager. It is very difficult to work with a client when he is weakening the document and yet he will not listen to your advice.

I also find that when I write for the CEO or the marketing departments, I have fewer edits. Make sure you have a clear idea of the company's culture and the purpose of the assignment. If you are able to present it well, they are unlikely to micromanage your work.

Realistically, you will find the average client has a few edits including some you may, or may not, agree with. A few will have no edits. On the other side of the coin, a few will be the clients I've described above. Know that this will happen, but don't dwell on it.

In freelance nonfiction writing, the product does not always end up being yours. If you know that going in, you will eliminate some unnecessary worry and reduce your frustration level.

In defense of the clients, you must make sure you are giving your best effort. You need to understand their wishes, write well, present error-free documents and use your creativity to design a document that will garner the reader's attention and interest.

It's a good way to earn money, but if you're a fiction writer, you need to understand the differences. I've collaborated with and trained writers who have never been exposed to this type of work. It's a lot like having a demanding English teacher and we can all remember those experiences -- except she usually improved our writing.

If you are freelancing and set up your own fees, make sure you bid enough time for edits. You will have to use the law of averages for this and you will learn by your own experience. An hourly rate is preferable to a flat fee, but many companies insist on the latter. If you have to quote a fee, figure in your writing and editing time. Otherwise, you may end up thinking you're working for minimum wage on some projects.

Hourly fees vary by your experience, the market, your geographic location and the project. You will need to check current writer's manuals or ask others in the field. If you are paid hourly, keep an accurate record of your time. Most companies are pretty savvy about the going rates and the amount of time required to complete a assignment.

THE WRITER'S PSYCHE

Get In Sync: How To Reach Your O.W.L. (Optimum Writing Level)

by Beverly Walton-Porter

Are you a morning lark or a night owl? Regardless of whether you favor early day or late night, to be the most productive writer you can be, you should work your writing into a scheme that will make use of the time of day when you have the largest burst of energy -- not just creative energy, but productive energy.

I'm a night owl and I admit it. My most creative moments occur when most people are drawing down the shutters and readying themselves for shut-eye. For years I've worked against this natural propensity to work late at night. Finally it dawned on me that I was working against my nature. I adjusted my work schedule as best I could, given the fact that I also have a family and since then I've produced more than I ever did. In short, I discovered my O.W.L. -- Optimum Writing Level.

Whenever possible, I try to do my research, interviewing and work-related reading during the day. Daytime is also when you can find me searching out new freelancing opportunities and making notes of where I need to send queries this coming week. When late afternoon rolls by, I stop and prepare dinner for my family. Then, once dinner is finished and all my other errands are covered, I then return to my home office to write.

This approach works for me since I can't think in a logical manner prior to ten am and without help from a pot of coffee. The downfall to all of this is that I do have a hard time shutting off my mind once I decide to get to bed for shut-eye. My mind is pumped up by then and continues to shoot images and ideas this-a-way and that.

Best way to calm those frenetic mental whirlwinds? Read. Yep. Read for enjoyment. Delve into some purely escapist literature. Soothing music is another cool down technique. My personal favorites are Yanni (don't laugh; even my kids calm down and conk out when they listen to his music!) or Enya. Perhaps you'll use some of those tapes with sounds of the ocean or a thunderstorm. You can find them close to the New Age section in the entertainment store. I have a tape of Jim Morrison and the Doors called An American Prayer in which Jim (who was a poet first before he was a singer) recites some of his work with the Doors' music as a backdrop. Whatever works, do it.

Getting to Know You

To thine own self be true, advised the Bard, William Shakespeare. Not bad advice; certainly a bonus for writers and poets. A definite must for freelancers. To work at your best level, you must first know yourself and your personal energy rhythms.

How to find your rhythm? Most people know whether they're more of a lark than a night owl or vice versa. You'll hear people say, "Oh, I'm up at the crack of dawn," or, "It takes me till late afternoon before I'm really cookin'." Take note -- which statement fits you the best? If you're still not sure, take a few days and make notes in your journal how you felt and what your energy level was in the morning, mid-morning, at lunch, in early afternoon, near dinnertime and late in the evening. Chances are, after studying your energy dips and peaks over several days you'll see a pattern emerging.

Now What?

You've determined your predominant energy cycle and personality, whether lark or owl. Now what? Think of how you can restructure your days and nights so you can write when you're at your best. This is known as O.W.L. (Optimum Writing Level), a little acronym I invented to label this marriage of writing when you're functioning at your highest peak of creativity/productivity.

Maybe you have excuses already: "Oh, there's no way I can write at five am" or, "All the good movies are on late-night TV." Sorry, but hardly any excuse is good enough. You want to write? Write. You will have to sacrifice something if you're serious about your profession. Late-night TV movies can be taped and if you're already up at five am, then there's no reason why you can't spend the time writing.

Give it a try and see for yourself. If there's a will, there's a way. Don't let the fear of the blank page keep you from writing early in the morning. Actually, writing when you first awaken is one of the best times to create. Your critic isn't quite awake yet and you'll get a chance to tap into the creative side of your brain. Julia Cameron, author of <u>The Artist's Way</u>, uses morning pages (writing three long-hand pages in the morning) as a way to connect with that essential, creative part of you.

In The Mood

Experts say it takes twenty-one days to change a habit. Now, I'm not sure how they arrived at the twenty-one day mark, but they're the experts, not me. Give your new writing schedule some time to sink in and attach to the walls of your psyche. Promise yourself a month's worth of experimentation.

To move yourself into your writing time and make it a recognizable habit, use an anchor -- something you do each time you begin your 'block' of prime writing time. For me, it's switching on the radio in my home office and pouring my cup of coffee. This puts me in the mindset that it's time to work.

Final Thoughts

Don't be impatient with yourself while you're discovering your O.W.L. You may have to rearrange your lifestyle a bit and do things you've never done before, but if in the long run that means becoming a more creative, more productive writer, then chances are, you'll be a happier writer.

We're all different, so work when your energy level is highest and don't try to imitate others. Morning lark? Night owl? One is no better than the other. The only thing that matters is how you use the self-knowledge you gain so you can become the most effective writer you can be.

first published at *Suite101* (www.suite101.com)

Using Emotions To Fuel Your Writing Fire

by Beverly Walton-Porter

Okay, so here you sit on another Tuesday night and you're wracking your brain for yet more potential query ideas to pitch to editors. There's only one problem: your gray cells have inched to the edge of your outer ear and they're threatening mutiny. You're blocked. You're disgusted. Your mind's a waste. You can't squeeze out another idea.

To put it bluntly – HOGWASH.

I once read an interesting book by Jean Marie Stine entitled <u>Double Your Brain Power - Increase Your Memory By Using All of Your Brain All The Time</u> This book gave no less than 66 brain-doubling exercises for readers to try out. The results are so quick that you'll wonder why you hadn't thought of some of these exercises sooner.

Relax. Scientists and other researchers unearthed these techniques. Hey, they have time to do neat stuff like think, whereas we overworked freelancers have to think, write, edit AND weep over rejection notices.

According to Stine's book, average humans such as ourselves have four thousand new ideas bombard us on a daily basis. Yet, as writers, we insist that we're occasionally afflicted with writer's block. What's going on here, Alfie? Shall we investigate this issue further?

Focusing Your Intent

If Stine's book and the studies she cites are correct, this means we're watching ideas go whizzing by our conscious like frenzied asteroids at a break-neck pace and with nary much of our attention focused on most of them. It's not that we aren't having ideas for articles or writing projects. It means we aren't focusing our intent enough to capture them and place them in the correct mental folder.

When we focus our intent and make a genuine effort to concentrate, we find ourselves able to think better, to produce more and to accomplish much more than we ever thought imaginable.

How Emotions Anchor Your Intent

No doubt about it, emotions serve as powerful fuel in our everyday lives. What's more, when we feel powerful emotions or emotional reactions to certain events or subjects, we tend to focus and concentrate more -- our intent is zeroed in and the awareness level is high. The high level of emotion connected to, or anchored to, a particular subject enhances our state of cognizance.

How can we couple this emotion/focusing of intent and harness its powers for our writing? How does this relate to us as writers? Simply put, we can manipulate and develop this supercharged emotional state of awareness and use this to draw forth reactions and questions we can explore further as potential article ideas.

Tapping Into Human Reactions And Emotions To Produce Ideas

By tapping into the current human condition and discovering what issues or events cause the public at large to react or recoil, freelance writers may find themselves tapping into a veritable well of potential article ideas that is never-ending.

If we suppose that we do, indeed, have four thousand unique thoughts each day, imagine how many query letters we can develop by using only ten percent of those daily thoughts and pitching only a small portion of those to editors. What makes the average human being tick these days? What's important to him or her? What delights, petrifies and enrages the senses?

Consider your own human reactions to recent events. Step out of your writer skin and tap into your emotional responses. Then focus your intent and your awareness on those issues. Jot down a quick, free-form list of your impressions or ideas.

Making a List and Fueling the Fire

Not sure how to begin? We'll take it step by step. You'll need a quiet environment. Some place where you can think and focus without distraction. Bring a notebook and a pen or pencil. If you can't find a quiet place in your home, take a walk in the woods or go for a drive.

Once you're in an environment conducive to concentrated, focused deliberation, pull out your paper and pen. Without hesitation, jot down a list of powerful emotions -- elation, rage, despair -- as many as you can describe, with a minimum of five to ten in your completed list.

Draw a line under each emotion. Now, look at the word. Focus on it. Feel the word. Say it out loud. Tap into how you react to the word and how, in past times or moments, you have experienced that particular emotion. Moreover, remember why you felt enraged and what the catalyst for the genesis of the emotion was.

For example, under "rage," you may recall a time when you felt as if you were consumed by an inner fire over an injustice you'd experienced. What was the injustice? Be specific. For instance, I remember experiencing an inner rage when I first discovered that baby seals were being clubbed to death. What human in his right mind could slaughter an innocent pup? I was more than angry -- I was enraged that such barbarism could occur.

Under "rage," my first entry would be: "baby seal clubbing." Then, I'd list one or two other issues whose injustices enraged me when I considered them. Next, move to your other emotion words and focus your awareness on each word and what it represents or has represented to you in your lifetime.

"Elation" may represent the sense of utter joy you felt when you won first place in a national sports event. "Despair" or "helplessness" might represent the depths you sank to when you discovered a close relative suffered from a terminal illness. Tap into the most powerful, comprehensive emotional moments you can muster. There is a method in this, I promise.

When you've completed your list of issues or events and matched them with their emotion words, now focus your intent on the results. Before you is an entire list of possible article ideas from which you can develop emotionally-absorbing, riveting pieces.

For example, has the clubbing of baby seals ended? If so, when? If not, why? More important, what can you, as a writer, find out about the subject and how can you develop the raw material into an issue worthy of print publication? Use your first draft list, polish and rework your emotionally-charged notes into potential query ideas and begin targeting publication markets that cater to such subjects.

Finally, this exercise could prove psychically, emotionally or spiritually exhausting for you if you're a sensitive individual. Emotions are powerful things -- and memories dredged up from within should be respected for what they are -- indelible blueprints of how you've lived, loved and learned in your lifetime.

Respect and honor your emotions, but at the same time, don't be afraid to use them to connect with readers on a deeper, more heartfelt level. Touch your readers inside and they'll never forget the imprint of your words. What better compliment can a writer receive than the approval of his or her audience?

first published at *Suite101* (www.suite101.com)

Writing and Mindfulness: Powerful Partners

by Mindy Phillips Lawrence

"When walking be conscious of the walking when writing be conscious of writing. Practicing thus, one lives in direct and constant mindfulness of the body." ~ Thich Naht Hahn, Vietnamese Buddhist monk

The computer on the desk is waiting. You are across the room staring at it, mind fractured into so many facets that ideas hit, bounce into the air and disperse. Yesterday you had a strong desire to write -- you had such creative thoughts. Where are those thoughts today when the moment comes to put them down?

We live in a world that asks us to multi-task. We answer the phone, wait on a customer and write notes at the same time without thinking about anything we have done. Five minutes later, we can't remember who called, who we waited on or what we wrote. No wonder the ideas that we appreciated last night have disappeared in the fog of morning.

Defining Mindfulness

We can bring our writing into focus by cultivating the Art of Mindfulness, moment-to-moment, non-judgmental awareness. We expand this gift in ourselves by refining our capacity to pay INTENTIONAL attention to the present moment, sustaining that attention over time to a greater and greater degree.

Mindfulness deals with the idea of "being present." Being present means performing a single task without thought to the next one. Nothing exists but the NOW.

Observation

Another aspect of mindfulness is observation, training your mind to observe without judging. You see the pen at your desk, you are aware of it, but you don't judge it. If you prefer a blue pen and the one you see is green, you accept the fact that the green pen in front of you is no less a pen and just as valuable.

Writing Mindfully

How does this help your writing? Let's think of it this way. If you weren't worried about whether you could pay the bills, whether or not the storm outside would blow you away, whether or not you would find the information you need for your article, whether or not you could finish writing it before the school bus gets home, how much better would your performance be? If all you were thinking of was your topic or the characters in your head and what they were saying to each other, how much easier would it be to transfer that topic or conversation to paper or computer? By breaking your day down into mindful segments, you can concern yourself with the act of writing when the time comes to write. It allows you to proceed moment-to-moment without thinking about the next task.

Cultivation

Mindfulness is a habit you can cultivate and expand over time. Be patient with yourself. Eventually, mindfulness will breed the patience you need for thoughtfulness and mental clarity. Don't become so eager to change your way of life that you think you can change your habits in a single day. Everything is progressive.

An Exercise in Mindfulness

✔ Before you begin to write, pause for a moment.

✔ Become aware of your body beginning at your toes and proceeding to the top of your head.

✔ Note any areas of tension, as in your shoulders or your face.

✔ Take a deep cleansing breath, blowing out the tension as you exhale.

✔ Scan your work area, becoming aware, but not concerned, with what is there and how it is arranged.

✔ Take another deep breath and let go of any concerns as you exhale.

✔ Take one more breath to center yourself.

✔ Slowly exhale.

✔ Begin your writing day.

Exercising the Writer's Soul -- Tai Chi

by Joyce Faulkner

I'm like that little girl on TV who loves bugs. I'm very passionate. Whereas that intensity translates into a pleasant rush for some, my obsessions take me to the edge of my last nerve. It was bad enough when I worked in the corporate world, but it worsened when I began writing full time from home where there are no external brakes.

As anyone who has ever dealt with me knows, it's grueling to be me. In fact, that's my picture you see in the dictionary under 'Type A'. Some days I write sixteen or seventeen hours out of the twenty-four -- sleeping only when my body refuses to function any longer. I've forgotten to take my medications on more than one occasion, gritting my teeth and holding my breath in an effort to force my blood pressure down to more acceptable levels. I've also forgotten to eat and gulped down OJ to keep from passing out when my blood sugar dropped. Heck, I've even sprained an ankle while sitting in my recliner.

Like other professions where hard work and discipline make the difference between success and failure, there are health risks associated with writing. Sitting in one position all day and night is not good for anyone. Add the potential for repetitive motion damage to the hands and arms from hours at the keyboard. Many of us have a tendency to eat too much or too little while working. Not enough exercise or sleep increases stress further. Mix in intensity -- that extra magic ingredient that makes our projects sparkle but can exhaust our bodies -- and you have a recipe for maladies like stroke, heart attack, arthritis, carpal tunnel syndrome and diabetes.

Exercise is an important tool in maintaining not just physical health but also mental acuity. Movement of any kind is good for those of us frozen in front of our desks. However, Tai Chi is a particularly good choice for writers. The movements are combined into several different routines or 'forms', the most popular being the 'short' form. Whereas

Westerners 'zone out' while running on a treadmill or pedaling a stationary bike, Tai Chi advocates exercise their minds and bodies at the same time. This causes blood to flow to the brain and stimulate the growth of neurons and tiny blood vessels.

One can view Tai Chi through several lenses. Some folks see it as 'moving yoga'. Others use it as an aid to meditation. Although it is a martial art, it is also a gentle exercise. What makes it so powerful is that just about everyone can do it. The elderly in managed care homes and people recovering from back and joint surgeries study it to recover their balance and strengthen their muscles. In my class, two people come and go with canes but are still able to keep up with the other students.

Philosophically, Tai Chi encourages an attitude where your mind and body are in harmony with each other. Steeped in the concept of give and take, the Yin/Yang symbol represents the Tao of Tai Chi -- a circle bisected by a wavy line, one side dark with a light dot, the other light with a dark dot. The two hemispheres are balanced. Simple though it may seem, the art form also embodies complexity and mystery. Verse 36 of the Tao states: "That which shrinks must first expand, that which fails must first be strong, that which is cast down must first be raised up." Tai Chi teaches you to relax and focus on dealing with the present -- which is the only thing you can control anyway. This is an ideal state of mind to be in while writing.

Tai Chi may take a lifetime to master, but one can accrue benefits quickly. From a personal perspective, it's about being relaxed and centered. From the standpoint of self-defense, it's about being strong enough to bend like a tree in the wind, using your opponent's power against him. From a writer's perspective, it's about allowing the ebb and flow of energy (Qi) to enhance your creative thinking.

Tai Chi has many benefits for sedentary people. Practitioners tend to have better muscle tone, improved breathing, more blood circulation, easier joint movement, increased flexibility, balance and coordination. Mentally, the exercises enhance concentration, body awareness and relaxation. They also relieve stress and build discipline -- important qualities for people who must sit down each day to a blank screen (or piece of paper).

There are practical considerations. First off, you don't need special clothes or shoes. You don't need to go to a gym to practice either. You don't need a lot of time -- it takes about eight minutes to perform the short form. Nor do you need a lot of space. You can buy new age music if that floats your boat, but it's not necessary. Ever the 'Type A', I practice in my kitchen right after I brush my teeth in the morning, after lunch and before bed. Ordinary folks put in thirty minutes of practice a day.

Although you get a good workout, you rarely break a sweat so don't worry about being stinky afterwards. The movements are slow and gentle and invigorating. I feel refreshed and ready to work when I'm done. If you are feeling strong, it's easy to incorporate Tai Chi with other forms of exercise like stretching, aerobics or weight training.

You can find Tai Chi courses in many of your local Martial Arts Studios and at community colleges or civic centers. Some companies hire instructors to lead employees in performing the short form at work. You can find seminars and workshops on the Internet. Cruise lines and spas offer classes. Groups of pajama-clad people do Tai Chi in city parks. Heck, just turn on the TV and watch the Celebrex commercial if all else fails.

I don't advocate learning Tai Chi from tapes or DVDs. Find a teacher because it's important to do the moves correctly and you need feedback from a real live person. However, for practice, there are several good DVDs on the market. Ask your instructor to recommend one.

first published at Scribe & *Quill* (www.scribequill.com)

Picture Yourself a Winner

by Pat McGrath Avery

Jack Canfield, the author of <u>The Success Principles and</u> other motivational speakers encourage us to create our vision, imagine ourselves achieving it and live accordingly.

That great advice can unleash creativity in a writer's mind. Let's imagine that your vision is to become a successful children's author. If this is your goal, you probably relate well to children. You most likely enjoy reading to them and telling them stories. Picture yourself in classrooms, libraries and bookstores observing the wonder on a child's face as he listens to you. Keep that face in your mind. Think about him every morning, during the day as you're working and last thing at night. Let that excitement symbolize your success.

Write your story for him. Multiply his face in your mind. Keep him personal, yet universalize his expression to every kid you see.

Visual reminders are valuable. Most of us learn and are motivated visually. Why else do we have pictures all over our houses including our refrigerator doors? If we're on a diet, we're told to 'think thin' and picture ourselves in sexy clothes. If we're out of shape, we're told to imagine ourselves as physically active and in shape.

Therefore, it makes sense that it will work for us as writers. If we create our vision, develop a strong picture of it in our minds, find and use visual reminders and keep it in our minds day and night, then we are impacting our futures in a very positive way.

If you realized how powerful your thoughts are, you would never think a negative thought. ~ Author Unknown

How many of you had parents or teachers who told you "you are who your friends are?" I heard that from my mother several times if she disapproved of a friend or a friend's actions. As a teenager, it made me mad; today it makes sense. In some ways, we become who we think we are and who we associate with. If we surround ourselves with successful and positive people, we will become successful and positive. What an important lesson to learn in life.

On the other hand, if we surround ourselves with people who have no dreams and ridicule ours, we find it much easier to sink toward their level rather than raise them to ours. Lack of dreams and goals has kept many 'wannabe' writers from becoming the real thing. It's hard work and it takes a vision, lots of discipline, a consistent writing schedule and getting involved in the industry.

Develop a plan. How many hours a day do you want to write? Make a schedule and stick with it. Everyone is busy and it's always hard to add something to our schedules. You know yourself. If you're a morning person, schedule yourself around your morning obligations. If you're a night person, do the same. I will never be the one who gets up an hour earlier and writes. However, I am the person who will stay up an hour later at night to get that time in. It takes a tremendous amount of discipline -- like diets and exercise. It has to become second nature to you -- as common and necessary as brushing your teeth.

Getting involved in writers and critique groups, attending conferences and making presentations are all part of a writer's life. These are excellent opportunities to learn and network. You can begin to brand yourself by taking part in activities. On the other hand, don't spend all your time attending meetings and conferences. Every event takes you away from writing. You will need to understand yourself and know the line between too many activities and not enough writing, or vice versa.

My philosophy is that not only are you responsible for your life, but doing the best at this moment puts you in the best place for the next moment. ~Oprah Winfrey

Most of us are fans of Oprah. She has created her own success and spent her energy helping others on their own roads to success. The best we are at any moment includes following our vision and helping others follow theirs.

Be willing to share yourself. You are unique. All of us are. You have learned and experienced things in your own unique way. If you are fortunate, you will find someone who will mentor you. In turn, you should mentor someone else. Their success becomes your success. There is no place for envy in the writer's world. Since each of us has our own writing voice and our own perception, there is room for all of us. Wish your fellow writer well. Those good wishes may just come back to you many times over.

I recently read the following story in My Daily Insights from AsAManThinketh.net. It was written by Jaroldeen Asplund Edwards and is presented here with permission.

Several times my daughter had telephoned, "Mother, you must come and see the daffodils before they are over." Finally, I promised, reluctantly. I'd driven only a few miles when the road was covered with wet, gray fog. As I executed the hazardous mountain turns, I was praying to reach the turnoff. When I finally walked into Carolyn's house, I said, "Forget the daffodils, Carolyn! There is nothing that I want to see bad enough to drive another inch in this weather!"

"I'll drive," Carolyn offered. In a few minutes, we were back on the Rim-of- the-World road heading over the top of the mountain.

We parked in a small parking lot adjoining a little stone church. I saw a pine needle covered path and an inconspicuous, hand lettered sign "Daffodil Garden." I followed Carolyn down the path. Then we turned a corner. It looked as though someone had taken a great vat of gold and poured it down every crevice and over every rise. Even in the mist, the mountainside was radiant, clothed in massive drifts and waterfalls of daffodils. A charming path wound through the garden with several resting stations, with Victorian wooden benches and great tubs of tulips. It didn't matter that the sun wasn't shining. Five acres of flowers!

"But who?" I asked Carolyn. "Just one woman," Carolyn answered. "That's her home. " On the patio we saw a poster. "Answers to the Questions I Know You Are Asking" was the headline. The first answer was simple. "50, 000 bulbs." The second was, "One at a time, by one woman, two hands, two feet and very little brain." The third was, "Began in 1958."

There it was. The Daffodil Principle. For me it was a life changing experience. I thought of this woman, who, more than thirty five years before, had begun one bulb at a time to bring beauty and joy to an obscure mountain top. No shortcuts, loving the slow process of planting. She had changed her world. Her daffodil garden taught me about learning to move toward our goals and desires one step at a time, learning to love the doing, learning to use the accumulation of time.

"It makes me sad in a way," I admitted. "What might I have accomplished if I had thought of a wonderful goal thirty-five years ago and worked away at it all those years. My wise daughter responded, "Start tomorrow."

Take one step at a time. Start today. It's good advice. We've heard it time and again. It is so pertinent to writers. How easy it is to procrastinate -- to wait until tomorrow, especially if we are not creatively energized today. However, discipline and dedication create their own energy and once we settle into writing, we can usually find something within ourselves. Sometimes, you'll write today and throw away tomorrow, but that's part of the game. Starting today is important in many ways including the following sobering thought.

We have no guarantee of tomorrow. If you dream of doing something, start today. ~ Author Unknown

INSPIRATION AND DISCIPLINE

The Complete Writer

Beat the Clock: Time Management for Writers

by Beverly Walton-Porter

What's the biggest excuse I hear from people who want to write, but don't? I'll bet you can already guess the answer: "But I don't have TIME to write!"

The concern is understandable. In today's society, forty hours of work per week has stretched to sixty, sometimes eighty and after work we have the kids' activities, community volunteer work and other obligations and concerns. Not having enough time seems to be an insidious disease wending its way through society's veins. We try to be all, do all, please all. Here's the problem -- we can't be/do/please all the time.

The Fallacy of "No Time To Write"

First of all, I believe that there is always a way to find time to write -- if you want to. Many people talk about writing and how they love to do it, but when it comes down to the bottom line, they aren't committed enough to carve out the time. If you want to meet any level of success with your writing, you have to do it.

When I worked full-time at a job other than writing, I had two breaks per day, plus a lunch hour. That added up to one hour and 40 minutes' worth of time when I could etch out writing time. Instead of using forty minutes of my break time sitting in the coffee room gossiping about who wore what today or who was having the biggest house built on the other side of town, I chose to read or write. "Read," you say? "Why, that's not writing." Ah, but when you read instructional books on writing, it is still doing the work. You read the book and then apply the principals learned therein.

During lunch hour, I would hop in my car and go have lunch by myself. I'd pull through the drive-thru of a fast food place and then park in an empty space in the lot to eat. After eating, I'd pull out my notebook and begin writing. If eating took me ten minutes, that still

90

gave me forty minutes to write and another ten minutes to return to work.

Did my reading/writing time pay off ? Resoundingly, "yes." That time spent reading, researching, learning and writing gave me a firm foundation and knowledge to strike out on my own and become a freelancer.

Managing to Find Time to Write

Aha. So you're thinking I meant something else by time management, huh? Maybe visions of daily planners rolling around in your head? The true element of time management is nothing more than taking an honest look at your schedule and deciding what you can do less of to write more. It also means using idle time doing something productive.

This is what I mean.

Television Time

How many hours a week do you spend watching television? You'd be amazed once you add it up. A couple hours each night multiplied by seven and you have fourteen whole hours you could've used to write. Okay, so you don't want to miss your favorite shows? Tape them and watch them after you've devoted yourself to writing at least an hour a day. If you cut back your TV viewing by half, that gives you much more time than you had before.

This is how I view television: it's an interesting medium, but unless it's educational TV or the news, I'm not very interested. If you're planning on writing a script for TV, I can understand why you might want to watch a ton of series or sitcoms. Otherwise, when you watch TV, make it more of a quality experience: watch public television, Discovery channel, The Learning Channel, The History Channel, Biography, A & E or any other station which offers informative programs that you can use as grist for the mill in your writing/creating.

Bottom line: if you're a TV junkie, cut your TV time at least in half to find time to write.

Idle Time

How do you spend your time when you're stuck waiting in the doctor's office or in the body shop customer center? This is idle time -- use it to write. Make a practice of carrying a small notebook and pen with you so you can pop it out at a moment's notice and jot down ideas or article outlines -- or begin an article.

Example: one year while returning home from a trip to a writers' conference in Kansas City, Missouri, I became bored as a passenger watching endless miles of asphalt race by outside the car window. Having just come off a writer's high from attending a conference with many published writers, I had an idea for an article.

I reached into my briefcase and found a small pad of yellow, lined paper and a pen. Within half an hour, I'd penned a rough draft of what eventually became "Eight Great Ways to Jump-start Your Writing." To date, that article has been reprinted more times than any of my other articles. The idea was hatched, then put in written form, during idle time. Time I would have otherwise spent watching flakes of snowing blow across cold asphalt on the way back home from Kansas City, Missouri.

Got idle time? Use it. Just because you're stuck waiting on something or somebody, that doesn't mean you can't make the best use of that time.

Claim One Special Writing Day for Yourself

Perfect timing for this topic. Why? Because the day after tomorrow is my birthday and I claim that as my day to do whatever I want (within reason, of course.) The gift I will give myself is the time to write whatever I want, just for that day. Maybe I'll decide to write haiku, although I haven't written haiku in ages. Maybe I'll decide to just write in a journal all day. Whatever I decide, it'll be my day and the gift I give to myself is the time to write without guilt or judgment.

Give yourself the gift of one special day to write -- but think in terms of every week. Then, once a year (perhaps on your birthday), give yourself the gift of one day of writing creatively in any form and about anything you want to write. Reconnect yourself with your love of writing. This is very important if you're a full-time or part-time freelancer. Why? Because you write for a living and it's easy to get away from writing just because you love to do it.

Don't be afraid to take the time to experiment. This year I'm going to experiment by beginning a children's book that's been stuffed down in my mind for most of the year. Will it sell? Who knows. Do I care? Nope. Why? Because I'm setting aside *my* special writing day to create something I want to try for the pure pleasure of it.

Prioritize

Writing has a priority in your life, but make sure it's ranked in the right spot. In the grand scheme of things, your family and duties as wife, husband, mother, grandmother, grandfather, etc. come before writing. Find a happy medium and stick with it. If that means you have to get up a little earlier or stay up a little later to fit writing into your home life, then so be it. You are entitled to writing time, but not to the detriment of your loved ones. You know what is reasonable and so do they.

This week, sit down and take a serious look at your lifestyle and the demands on your time. Grab a piece of paper and work it out in black and white. Where are the spaces that can be filled with writing? What activities are you willing to curtail or eliminate in favor of stalking your dream and making it reality? Remember, writing doesn't just happen; you have to make the commitment and take daily steps if you intend to meet and exceed the personal writing goals you've set for yourself.

first published at *Suite101* (www.suite101.com)

Eight Great Ways To Jump-Start Your Writing

by Beverly Walton-Porter

It's unwelcome, but inevitable: someday you'll face the dreaded affliction known as "writer's block." This damnable malady may wreak havoc on your creativity for a day, week or month but you don't have to be a willing victim. You can combat and conquer it with these eight sure-fire remedies designed to crank up your creative urges and jump-start your writing. Guaranteed.

1. Start a Dream Diary

Some of the best "scenes" and story lines come are those which spring unbidden from the deepest recesses of your unconscious mind. If you're not inclined to snapping on the night light to scribble down the remnants of a fast-fading dream, buy an inexpensive compact tape recorder and record your impressions upon awakening.

If you're unable to recall every last tidbit of your dream, don't fret. Just as snippets of newspaper articles can be used as a catalyst for your next story, dream snippets can provide unique bits and pieces which can be woven together later on to spice up plots, characters or spark ideas for nonfiction articles.

2. Keep a Journal

Keeping a journal is one of the most effective ways of combating writer's block. Make your journal as nonrestrictive and nonthreatening as possible. No one will be sitting behind your shoulder counting off points for grammar, punctuation or paragraph structure. Silence your inner critic and write about what you're sensing or experiencing. Are you angry? Sad? Euphoric? Why? Be as specific and descriptive as possible. Don't set limits on the frequency or length of your entries; instead, concentrate on consistently writing in your journal.

A word of advice: although some writers use computers for journaling, the aesthetic experience of journaling with good, old-fashioned pen and paper appeals more to the writer within me. It's your choice, but regardless of your preference, the basic idea is to give your creative self free rein. You may be hard-pressed to sit down "cold" and produce the first chapter of your book, so allow yourself a "warm up" by journaling.

3. Buy a Book of Baby Names

The purchase of a pocket book of baby names can not only be a tool in naming your next character, it can also be used as a way to recharge your imagination. Each week, choose a name or two from the book and develop a character sketch out of the impressions you receive from saying and thinking about the name you've chosen. What would this person look like? What personality traits would they possess? Who are their relatives and what are their names? Where would a person named Beauregard be born and under what circumstances? How would they dress and what foods would they prefer?

Whether you've chosen Maribelle or Myrtle, develop a person from that name using your impressions and personal poetic license. The stable of characters you create can then be used to people your upcoming short stories or novels and the plot twists will evolve naturally from your characters' flaws and weaknesses.

4. Expand Your Powers of Observation

If you're not already an avid people watcher, become one. Begin ferreting out expressions and mannerisms of members of the general public engaged in daily activity. Note any habits that could be used as an effective "tag" for your fictional characters. Carry a small notepad and record not only people's characteristics or witticisms, but the surroundings. People tend to behave differently depending on whether they're attending church or attending a football game.

Jot down the flora and fauna of your hometown surroundings or any area you visit. Observe the similarities of people living in small towns, mid-sized cities or large, urban areas. Use these simple notes and observations as a springboard for setting in your next story.

Although your fictional setting may not be real, you can fool your reader into believing there is a place by adding authentic sights, sounds and smells borrowed from your people/place-watching notes.

5. Brainstorm/Free-Associate

Brainstorming and free-association ranks at the top of effective ways to energize your brain cells into a more inventive mode. Allow yourself five minutes to jot down any words that come to mind. Put your pen to paper (or your fingers to keyboard) and write as many as you can within the time allotted. Don't allow your internal critic to censor anything -- write every single thing that pops into your mind.

That done, take an additional ten minutes and read each word you wrote down, writing the first words that come to mind when you go back over your initial list. Don't just shoot for associated words, dig deeper into your subconscious and give voice to any impressions you receive. Once your time is up, study the words you've culled from your subconscious. Are there any obvious story lines or characters ?

Play the "what if" game with each of the words. Pair the words together, using different combinations to spark your imagination. Then repair them, using the resulting combinations as a beginning for a whole new range of plot/character possibilities.

6. Cut It Out

Cut pictures, photographs and headlines from magazines and newspapers. Anything that strikes your fancy or piques your curiosity should be perfect targets for clipping. Use people or objects or beautiful scenery that inspires you. Add your collection of clippings to a large basket or box and randomly withdraw five clippings.

Use the clippings to develop a story, asking yourself who, what, why, where, when and how. Who is the little girl in the picture and where are her parents? What is her hometown like and how long has she lived there? When is she due home for dinner and why is she happy/sad in the picture?

7. Give Yourself A Working Vacation

Once a week, spend a single day writing for nothing but pleasure. Forget about deadlines, query letters, synopses, proposals, word processors and spell checkers. Get back to the basics and immerse yourself in writing for the sheer pleasure and nothing more. Grab a pen and paper (no computers allowed) and empty your mind, allowing the images to flow freely.

Stymied by sonnets? Have a hankerin' for Haiku? Mystified by meter? If you've never penned a poem, here is your chance to throw caution to the wind and do it. Ever wondered if you could write a screenplay in the proper format? This is the day for you to experiment and stretch your writing muscles. Any piece of work you produce on this day is for your eyes only, unless you decide otherwise.

The point is to allay yourself of any pressure to perform, to allow your inner muse to blossom and expand in any writing area (familiar or foreign) you wish. To write for nothing more, nothing less, than the pure pleasure of the act.

8. Relax, Don't Do It

Sometimes one learns to do by not doing. Meditation, creative visualization and guided relaxation may sound like New Age buzzwords to the practical, no nonsense writer, but any or all of the above can help your writing performance. Go to the local library or bookstore and check out the latest books on relaxation. Just as an athlete's body needs cooling down after it's been stretched to its physical limits, we as writers need a mental "cool down".

Choose one day a week to relax by taking a walk, meditating or utilizing creative visualization. Allow your mental processes time for recuperation. If you're using creative visualization, see yourself as successful and productive; explore the feeling finding a check in the mailbox instead of a rejection letter. Let your mind conjure up as many positive, reinforcing images of writing as you can. See yourself in your own mind and notice how confident and optimistic you are, excited to send off that next book proposal or query letter. Envision how relaxed your shoulders and neck feel; in you, there is no tension, no anxiety. You are a writer; you are doing what you love.

first published at *Suite101* (www.suite101.com)

Driven To Distraction – Moving From Unfocused To Focused

by Beverly Walton-Porter

On line role-playing games. Solitaire. Minesweeper. Scrabble. Ebay auctions. www.bored.com. Obscure facts and figures you'll never need to know. What do all these things have in common? They're all things that have caused me to veer off the writing path and become unfocused.

Yes, it's true. I'm not the perfect freelancer. I, too, have my downfalls. One of which is an overactive mind that tends to flit and light upon twenty bazillion things in a matter of minutes. I drink coffee to slow my mind down and focus more.

Although I thought I was the only one with this nagging problem, one fine day I received an e-mail message from a good friend of mine who is also a full-time freelance writer. What'd she want to know? Why, she wanted to know if I ever had a problem with becoming distracted while working on an article.

I was shocked to receive her message and even more shocked to discover she'd admitted this to me at all. This particular friend is, quite simply, the "perfect" freelancer, in my eyes. In my mind, she was never distracted, she never dealt with writer's block and she was able to leap incredible deadlines in a single bound. In short, my friend symbolized the type of freelancer I hope to emulate. Imagine my surprise when I received her confessionary e-mail.

Is confessionary a word? No matter ... I think you know what I mean. Besides, I'm too focused to look up the answer -- or too lazy, I'm not sure which. The thing is this: don't feel guilty if your mind does wander on occasion. One thing we must remember is that, as writers, our profession is very thought-intensive. Instead of building structures with our hands, we build word structures with our minds. As any student of meditation will tell you, the mind loves to wander and often fights when told to focus and settle itself.

To get our minds to focus more, we must play "Let's Make a Deal." We need to tell our minds, "Hey, I have to get this work done, but you're getting into that wanderlust mood again -- right when I have a deadline." So, you make a deal. That's right, you're Monty Hall and your mind is the contestant. You whisper in your contestant's ear: "Psst! Hey, you! If you'll give me your undivided attention for a few hours, then we'll have a little play time and you can do whatever you want"

Being the unruly child your mind can often be, your mind perks up and considers the deal. "You mean if I give you a few hours of time, you'll get off my back and let me have some freedom *not* to think/analyze/create for a while?" You nod sagely, knowing it takes a clever freelancer to come to terms with the sometimes-disobedient mind.

Okay, so maybe I'm exaggerating a bit -- but not by much. Our minds are powerful tools and freelancers much learn to harness the power of this amazing tool while respecting its need for rejuvenation. All work and no play is never a good equation. It leads to burnout, resentment and decreased productivity. If you don't give your mind time to wander and play, it'll pay you back one way or another.

Now that you know that I'm not the perfectly focused freelancer you thought I was, we can work on this problem together. I can't promise I'll never be distracted by Cosmo's Conundrum again, but I can promise to work on it.

With that in mind, here are five tips for moving from unfocused to focused. I'll make you a deal: you practice these for the rest of this week and I'll do the same. After I get my last dose of Cosmo, that is.

Five Steps for Corralling the Free-roaming Freelancer Within

1. Respond to social e-mail after your work is done for the day. I know this may be a difficult nut to crack -- but we have to try and knuckle down on this ultimate time-waster. Addicted to e-mail? Yep, that's me. Got a neat self-test or joke to spread my way? Send it on over, Red Rover. Unfortunately, social e-mail takes a huge bite out of writing time and also uses up that creative energy you should be using on the articles, stories or

poetry instead. To curb the urge to respond to e-mail throughout the day, make a pact with yourself that you will only respond to e-mail that is work-related during your regular freelancing hours. E-mail which is important, but not work-related, is next in line, then social e-mail comes last. After you've finished your assignments for the day, then treat yourself to an hour of time when you read and respond to nothing but fun/social e-mail with friends or family. By drawing this boundary, you won't mix the two and find yourself stuck in the Web of e-mail that will sap your work and work energy. If you don't want to go through your whole workday without giving yourself an e-mail break, then segment your time into work/play boundaries. For instance, if you work eight A.M. to five P.M., etch out eight A.M. to twelve noon for work. Then, leave your desk, take a half hour for lunch and devote a half hour to catching up on e-mail that is not related to work, but is still important and requires an answer. At one P.M., resume freelance work until 4:30 P.M., then use your last half hour for responding to more e-mail.

2. Don't play games until after the work is complete. E-mail is one thing, blowing four hours on on line games is quite another. On line games can be addictive and if you're not careful, they can become akin to a mental black hole if you're not careful. Save the games until after your work is done for the day. You must be firm on this, above all else. Make this a treat to yourself for putting in a good day's work or tackling a huge assignment. Promise yourself some mental recreation once the hard work's through and you'll appreciate it that much more.

3. Save the surprises for last. That means the current condition of your Ebay auction account and your stock portfolios or anything else you might be gauging. You don't need to know all the information all the time throughout the day. Play a game with yourself and see if you can guess the results at the end of the day -- and wait until before bedtime to check those results. Anticipation can be sweet, after all.

4. The Web has more strange, esoteric and intriguing sites than you'll ever be able to see in your whole life. If you want to go wandering the Web, please make sure your wanderings have a purpose during times when you're researching an article. Otherwise, reserve specific daily blocks of time or weekends for pleasure surfing. Not only will you be happy with your newfound commitment to focused surfing, you'll begin to look forward to weekends as the time when you're free to seek out the wild fruits of the Web without your conscience nagging the heck out of you.

5. Realize you're a human being, not a robot. As soon as you embrace this fact, you'll be much happier. The very thing that makes us writers is the very thing that can draw our focus away. We are creative beings, but within that freedom of creativity also comes the need for boundaries.

It's true that I'm not a master yet, but I know I've come a long way since I began. For most of us human beings, that's all we can ask. We continue to work and improve until we meet our goal. I know I won't give up. How about you?

first published at *Suite101* (www.suite101.com)

RESEARCH AND ORGANIZATION

The Complete Writer

I Am Your Computer: Speak To Me -- Boolean Searches

by Joyce Faulkner

I am your new computer. Click. Beep. Not one of those old fashioned jobbies that takes up half your desk, but a slim-profiled one you can hold in your lap. Purrr. We are going to be oh so very close. I am the perfect slave -- I'll do anything you ask whether you mean it or not. I'll do it over and over again till you tell me to stop. I never get tired. I don't mind if you yell at me. I'll love you till I die -- or you trade me in for a newer model, whichever comes first.

You keep a list of your favorite DVDs on me. You can have them back whenever you want. In any order. You can look for your favorite Eastwood flick or find all the Kevin Bacon movies you own. All you have to do is talk to me. In my language. After all, I can't read your mind.

Where I come from, a question is called a query. I know that distresses you. Get used to it, lover. I'll make it worth your while. George Boole taught me to respond. He was a square-jawed Englishman back in the good old days before I was invented. Not as cute as little Billy Gates -- but not bad. He came up with a branch of mathematics called 'symbolic logic'. The guys who built me used old George's "Boolean" logic to whisper in my ear. It suits the way I think -- black and white, off and on, zero and one. Crisp. Clean. Precise.

Uncle George came up with a way to sort through my data using words like 'AND', 'OR' and 'NOT'. They are called Boolean Operators. Like bon-bons soften up your other lovers, these special commands are the keys to my heart -- helping me decide which bit of information matches your request.

If you want to see all the Clint Eastwood films that are westerns that do not also star Gene Hackman, I'll be glad to present them to you if you ask me right. Until we see eye to eye, it might take you several tries though. You need to know what you want. For example, if you type in "Eastwood", I'll give you every single record I have on file pertaining to "Eastwood" -- including 'Eastwood Drive' and 'Elmo Eastwood' from Trenton. When you yelp and scratch your head in aggravation, my screen will flicker impassively -- waiting for your next query. I gave you what you asked for, after all.

Perhaps you try, "'Eastwood' OR 'westerns'", the next time around. To me, OR means "I want documents that contain EITHER word." Ahhh! You want MORE data. Whirrrrr! I spew out hundreds of records -- all the ones from your first query along with all the westerns in your collection -- whether Clint starred in them or not. Whether Gene starred in them or not. It's no skin off my hard drive if you pull your hair and gnash your teeth.

You set me on the seat of your recliner and pace back and forth, thinking. I take a picture of you with smoke coming out your ears and your finger in the 'AHA' position. You tap in, "'Eastwood' AND 'western'". That tells me you want ONLY records that contain BOTH words. My hard drive hums. There ya go, sweety. A much smaller list. You see your own gold tooth reflected in my screen. Uh oh. 'Unforgiven' is shown. Gene Hackman. Your grin fades. You yank out my mouse and throw it against the wall. Don't try that with ME, bub! I freeze and you are done for the day.

The next morning you buy me a new mouse and I roar back to life, yesterday's unpleasantness swept from my RAM memory. Beep. Hello, big boy. You consult Uncle George's theories in your freshman algebra text. Your fingers caress my keys. "'Eastwood' AND 'western' AND NOT 'Hackman'." PERFECT. I know what to do. I start at the top of the list. Does the first record have the word 'Eastwood'? No. I move to the second document. Does it have the word 'Eastwood'? Yes. Does it have the word 'western'? Yes. Does it have the word 'Hackman'? No. Eureka! I pick that one and go to the next -- 'In the Line of Fire.' It has the word 'Eastwood' but it's not a western. I skip it and go to the next -- 'Play Misty For Me'. The name of each movie that meets all the criteria scrolls across my screen. I play a celebratory tune and you dance a jig. We are in love again.

Of course, our relationship becomes more intense when you are writing. Perhaps that's because your needs are greater. You surf the net with grim determination. You scan the archives of subscription services. You pound on my keys, gazing into my screen with your mouth agape. You don't have to be such a brute as my old friend Sylvia would say, but I forgive you with the fervor of a fasting monk. Whether you are probing my databases or those of my sisters linked through the Internet, Uncle George's principles will translate your demands into queries that elicit reliable responses from me.

Boolean searches have become an important tool for writers. Here's a list of web sites that describe in varying degrees of complexity what it takes to communicate your desires to me.

http://library.albany.edu/internet/choose.html

http://www.nyu.edu/library/bobst/info/instruct/tutorials/
    boolean/boolean.html

http://searchenginewatch.com/facts/boolean.html

At the end of a long day, as I lie warm and pulsing in your lap, you slip a DVD into my drive and we cuddle like lovers do. The movie starts. 'Absolute Power'. YIKES. Gene Hackman is the president? You pat the edge of my screen. I could have found that for you, you know. Beep. Whirrr.

first published at Scribe & Quill (www.scribequill.com)

Where To Go When You Need To Know -- Searching the Internet -- The Basics!

by Joyce Faulkner

To be a writer one has to be part private detective, part librarian and part mole. Ferreting out intriguing stories, unknown facts and interesting people is your stock in trade. In the last fifteen years, the Internet has become an informational cornucopia available anytime of the day or night. It provides access to enumerable databases both public and private, for free and for fee. The trick is to know how to find what you want.

Search Engines are programs that scan subject web sites and compile them into indexes. They use algorithms -- specific criteria to sort and rank the content. Users then create 'queries' to retrieve lists of Hyperlinks to the sites that best answer the question. Cool, right? There is a caveat. Search Engines can't insure quality or truth. Anyone can create a web site and publish pretty much anything they want on it. Web material can be influenced by politics, religion, geography, culture, individual bias and flat out ignorance. Deliberate hoaxes and realms of misinformation abound.

Keeping that in mind, search engines are a terrific way to collect a lot of information on the cheap. I have included some of my favorite ones below.

- ✔ www.yahoo.com

- ✔ www.askjeeves.com

- ✔ www.google.com

- ✔ www.lycos.com

Here are a few tips on using them effectively.

1. Understand Boolean Logic. Dig out your algebra books and

refresh yourself on the meanings of AND and OR in particular. This basic knowledge will also help you when searching private databases and library archives.

2. If a search engine provides you with an advanced option, use it. It will narrow your search and reduce your wandering around time.

3. If you surround your request with quotes, the engine will search for the sequence of words included in your query. For example, if you type "Amazon Cruises" into the search box, the program will return only those pages that feature the words "Amazon Cruises" in that order. On the other hand, if you type in Amazon Cruises, you will get pages with the word 'Amazon' AND pages with the word 'Cruises' AND pages with the words 'Amazon Cruises' AND pages with the words 'Cruises Amazon'. As you can imagine, you'll find yourself slogging through a lot more irrelevant pages with the second approach.

4. Search algorithms change frequently. This is because search engines try to be 'fair' while web sites want to 'cheat'. (As an example, an early algorithm counted the number of times a key word appeared in the text of a page. The pages that used that word the most ranked higher on the result list. As a cheating Webmaster, I repeated my key words in white on a white background hundreds of times. Apparently, I wasn't the only one who tried that tactic and the algorithm was changed.) This means that the ranking may or may not relate to your idea of what's most important.

5. Statistically, most people review one page of search results, many go through the second page but very few go beyond three. I recommend either narrowing your search through Boolean techniques OR browsing deeper than the norm. That is, check the one-hundredth page or the one-thousandth. What you are seeking might be buried that far back.

6. Use multiple search engines. Although you might end up with the same material, the ranking may be different (saving you

from spending time browsing deeper in the search results) or some pages may not be included in all search algorithms. Some search engines have a programmatic 'robot' that goes out and searches the web to find new sites or incorporate changes into the index. Others require site owners to register. Still others require web sites to 'bid' or pay for a prominent ranking.

7. You can use search engines in surprising ways. For example, if you know a person's telephone number but want to know their e-mail address (or if you suspect that a person has not given you their correct name), you can type the telephone number into the search box. Sometimes, people will post to newsgroups using signature files that include their real phone numbers. Remember to try all the different formats: '(xxx) xxx-xxxx', 'xxx-xxx-xxxx', etc.

8. Some search engines allow you to use 'wild cards' in the search box. This expands your query. For example, suppose you want to find all those pages with 'Faulkner', 'Faulk' and 'Faulkner'. You could type in 'Faulk*' and the program will return all those pages with words beginning with "Faulk"

9. Many search engines indicate the area of search. For example, www.mamma.com allows you to search the 'web' or 'news' or 'images' or 'audio' or a specialized category for 'kids'. If you type 'Mondale' into the 'web' section, you will get historical and analytical information about your subject. If you type 'Mondale' into the 'news' section, you are more likely to get information about his recent senate race. If you type 'Mondale' into the images section, you are going to get photographs and if you go for the 'audio' section, you will retrieve audio files of his speeches.

10. Many search engines are also directories. That is, information is organized so that you can burrow down from the general to the specific. An example of this kind of search facility is www.yahoo.com. They have fourteen main categories and many subcategories. If you are interested in finding a page on 'quotations', you can browse through a link called 'Reference' to a second page that lists forty additional links – one of which

is 'Quotations'. You can choose from one hundred, eighty-eight individual links in that subcategory.

11. Some search sites act as portals with auxiliary functions such as finding names, addresses, e-mail addresses, phone numbers, etc for both individuals and companies. Here are a few alternative sites which offer more specific searches.

PHONE NUMBERS:

http://www.teldir.com

http://peoplesearch.net

http://www.anywho.com

LIBRARIES:

http://www.libraryspot.com

http://www.ala.org/alonline

http://www.archives.gov/welcome/index.html

http://sunsite.berkeley.edu/Libweb

NEWSPAPERS:

http://www.onlinenewspapers.com/

http://www.ipl.org/div/news/

http://www.newspapers.com/

first published at *Scribe & Quill* (www.scribequill.com)

Magazines On the Cheap

by Mindy Phillips Lawrence

When you are searching for writing markets, how many times do you see wording similar to this -- *We hope you will look over several issues of our magazine to get an idea of the range and style of articles we publish?*

Where does a writer get all those magazines? When submission guidelines request reading three or four issues before sending a query, how can a struggling writing afford that many subscriptions? What's a writer to do?

How about getting magazines on the cheap? Magazines are everywhere. All money-strapped writers have to do is know where to hook up with the supply. After talking to several writers, here are some of their sources for magazines that cost little or nothing.

Half-price or second-hand bookstores

When you think of half-price and second-hand bookstores, you think of, well, BOOKS -- but many also have magazines available. Find a business like this in your area and talk to its owner. See what magazines wind up there and if these are the ones you want. If not, ask the owner to let you know when a new supply comes in. Take a few business cards and tell your friends about the bookstore. Help the owner a little while she helps you.

Internet/E-Bay

What did we ever do without the Internet? Many magazines are now on line with free issues. Search for their web sites and bookmark them. You can read published articles and often find a list of pending articles. Look at the types and topics covered and mimic them.

The Internet also has auction sites like E-Bay and Yahoo Auction. Find what's offered under magazines and bid low. You win some, you lose some, but it's fun either way.

Libraries

Having a library day is a good idea. If you work a full-time job (which most writers do), set part of your Saturday aside and go to the library. You can check out magazine issues and get a list from the circulation desk of the magazines the library carries. Don't forget to check out both public AND college libraries. Their available selections will be different -- and all for the cost of a library card.

If a magazine you want is not in your library, ask about it. Enlist your friends by having them call the library and ask for the same magazine. Many libraries choose their acquisitions based on demand.

Writers' groups

Writers groups can also share what they have. Members can bring their magazines to meetings for trade. Set up a table and pile the magazines on it. At a break, before or after the meeting, let the members select several different magazines to take home. Suggest they recycle these back to the group when they are done.

A magazine-sharing circle (I have one subscription, you have one and someone else has another). Most writers have friends who are writers. Why not start a magazine-sharing circle? You get one or two subscriptions and someone else gets subscriptions to other magazines. Get a group together and share, share, share.

Friends and relatives

A mother, sister, brother, aunt, grandmother or best friend – all subscribe to different magazines. If you are writing for a younger audience, ask your son or daughter for the magazines they've been reading (this is also a way to get your pulse on what's selling to a given audience). Borrow returning issues if your friends and relatives are partial to what they have and want to keep their issues. Otherwise, collect, collect, collect.

Waiting rooms

Think of the waiting rooms where you sit before an appointment and read magazines lying around. Sometimes the issues are not new but still current enough to be interesting. Why not ask the receptionist if you can borrow a few in exchange for bringing in newer issues as you finish with them? You will make other patients a little happier and get the magazines you want for free.

Don't just think doctors and dentists. Also think industrial and client waiting rooms where you conduct business. If you wander through a hospital, grab the hospital's in-house magazine. It's usually free -- and a market in itself.

Humane Society

The Humane Society usually has a shop that sells items to make money for the shelter. Ask if your area society offers magazines. For a few dollars, you can often buy bundles of magazines and donate to a good cause at the same time. If your local society doesn't do this, why not encourage them to start? Tell them you will lead all your writer friends to their door. Who knows? Maybe a friend will also take home a literary dog or cat.

Salvation Army or Goodwill

Similar to the Humane Society, the Salvation Army and Goodwill sometime have magazines in bulk to sell for next to nothing. Again, if they haven't thought of this for themselves, put a bug in their ear and tell them you will send your writer friends to look at their merchandise and magazines.

Sample subscriptions

This method of acquiring magazines takes a bit of attention to detail. Many credit cards offer sample subscriptions. You receive a month or two of certain magazines and, if you don't want to keep the subscriptions, the credit card company removes the payment from your credit card. You MUST pay close attention to when the sample subscriptions are due to run out and make sure they are not charged to you card. Keep good records.

Searching for cheap, useful magazines is like a treasure hunt. You never know where you might find helpful issues as you go through your day. See if your office will start an exchange. Trade in small numbers of frequent flyer miles for subscriptions. Check high and low and get those queries in the mail.

first published at Scrib*e & Quill* (www.scribequill.com)

Load Up On Valuable E-mail Goodies

by Pat McGrath Avery

Do you think you already get too many e-mails? For what seems like many years now, I've been dutifully checking my e-mail several times a day for business communications. Yet I recently discovered I've been missing some of the best materials available.

I thought I didn't have time for a lot of newsletters and e-mails, but after being encouraged by friends to sign up for a couple, I've found they are great assets. All of the e-zines mentioned below are free. Many of the publishers also offer paid newsletters with more in-depth content.

As writers, we have several constant needs; one is motivation and another is information. So if you're not an e-newsletter or e-zine enthusiast yet, I suggest you start looking into those two areas.

I receive several daily motivational letters -- short and sweet, but they start your day off right. It's easy to think you're getting nowhere in your writing career. However, a daily dose of motivational medicine goes a long way to keeping the fire burning and the spirit healthy.

I'm going to mention a few, but you will find dozens of them if you do an Internet search. I like www.myfavoriteezines.com published by Sharon Iezzi. It's delivered three times a week with motivational materials. *My Daily Insight*, www.motivational-inspirational-corner.com and www.motivateandinspire.com have daily motivational quotes you can receive through a free subscription. I also enjoy Steve Goodier's newsletter. Subscribe to it through www. life supportsystem. com.

Okay, now you're motivated, so let's get some good information about writing. *Scribe & Quill* (www.scribequill.com) publishes an excellent newsletter. Author interviews, book reviews and articles on writing are all included in each issue. I also like the newsletter from www.fundsforwriters.com, offering different newsletters based on the size of the markets. It lists a variety of paying markets and contests for writers.

If you like to read about new books, subscribe to the Curled Up With a Good Book newsletter at www.curledup.com or check out the book reviews and entertainment news at www.TheCelebrityCafe.com.

Many writers today have taken on the added responsibility of self-publishing. If you have an interest in that side of the market, there are some excellent newsletters you will need to read. Dan Poynter is one of the gurus in the field and he offers an excellent e-zine, *Your Publishing Poynters*, which is available from www.danpoynter @parapublishing.com. RJ Communications offers *Publishing Basics* featuring various experts. Sign up through www.booksjustbooks.com.

Two organizations, SPAN (Small Publishers of North America) and SPAWN (Small Publishers, Artists and Writers Network) offer free e-newsletters to non-members. Check out SPAN at www.spannet.org and SPAWN at www.spawn.org. Both give lots of valuable information.

Brian Jud, a marketing expert, offers a free e-zine, *Book Marketing Matters*, filled with advice from other experts in the field. Check out www.bookmarketing.com. John Kremer, author of <u>1001 Ways to Market Your Books</u>, publishes a free e-zine available at www.bookmarket.com. Joan Stewart, a publicity expert, publishes *The Publicity Hounds Tips of the Week*, available through www. thepublicityhound. com.

To keep abreast of publishing happenings, check out *Publishers Lunch* from www.publishersmarketplace@yahoo.com. They publish daily, with both a free and a paid version. The paid version contains more detailed information.

Peter Bowerman, author of <u>The Well-Fed Writer,</u> suggests keeping all e-mails for later use. I have done this with the quotes, motivational materials and writing information. However, he suggests you go a step further, keeping every joke and story that you receive. Make them into a database of material that you can use in your writing and in your presentations. Great idea. I intend to keep everything. As I understand it, once you archive e-mail it no longer uses up your space.

We're not that far removed from the days when all our resources were printed materials. What an easy way we have to store things today. It's so much easier to sort through e-mail folders than boxes or files containing all sizes of papers, post-it notes, napkins and the like. That's not to say I still don't use the old method for ideas and information that I find outside my friendly computer. It's that I've passed the stage where I had to print out everything.

Please realize that I've given you just a minute sampling of the e-zines that are out there to help you as a writer. Once you start reading a few, you will find many more. Check out a lot of them, then settle in to the ones that most inspire and guide you.

Traveling for Research (Part One) -- Planning

by Joyce Faulkner

You've decided to set your novel in Key West because your main character is a sponge fisherman. Okay. That sounds exciting. The only problem is that you've never been in Florida. Oh, there are maps and photographs to be found on line. You can rent movies like "Beneath the Twelve Mile Reef" or buy Hemingway's "To Have and Have Not." That kind of research is important, but it's only part of the story – filtered through someone else's soul.

How will you know how it feels to stand on Mallory Square and toast the sunset? How will you know about the man with the pale yellow snake who stands in front of the trinket booths on Duval Street? How will you know about the haunted Bed and Breakfast on Eaton Street? How will you know the thousands of tiny details that might influence your story if you don't visit that beautiful and bizarre bit of paradise at the southern point of the United States?

For many of us, travel is a crucial part of the research process for our writing projects. It's where we find plots and subplots, characters, background images and history. Although it can be expensive and time-consuming, it enriches your work as nothing else can.

To make the most of the experience, I try to achieve a balance between planned activities and spontaneous adventures. The very first thing I do is determine what my budget is going to be and how much time I'm going to be able to spend at the location in question. This helps me set the realm of possible and establish priorities.

I do a significant amount of work on the book before I plan the trip. I may not know much about the locale I am considering, but I do have a loose idea of my plot. Then I make a list of information I want to collect. Things like: architecture of the area, newspaper clippings from the time frame in question, local history and background stories, local dialects, local "looks", layout of the town, schools, etc.

Generally, at this stage, I make use of www.Google.com and www.AskJeeves.com. I read any web sites about the area I can find, following the links to recommended Hotels, Bed & Breakfast Inns or tours. I also make a trip to a bookstore (no www.amazon.com this time) and thumb through the various travel guides available to get a feel for what is available in the city of interest.

When I went to Key West, for example, I was looking for a house where my characters would take shelter during a hurricane. I wanted it to be close to the center of town, I wanted my characters to be able to land at the dock and walk to their rooming house. I wanted it to be close to a local watering hole. Therefore, where we stayed was very important – and I spent money as was appropriate to find a Bed and Breakfast that resembled the place I had in mind. When I went to Auschwitz to research another novel, I knew that the hotel had nothing to do with the story I wanted to tell so where we stayed wasn't important.

When possible, I find a travel agent who is sympathetic to my needs and who is willing to give me input. For example, I wanted to see Key West from the air and mentioned that I'd like to do a bit of flying. My travel agent then made two suggestions that turned out to be critical to the plot of my story. One was to take a seaplane tour out to Fort Jefferson. The other was to go up in an old WACO biplane at sunset. Hotel concierges can play the same role.

I take as many tours as possible. In Key West, we took walking tours, shuttle train tours, airplane tours and kayak tours. Each one added to my understanding of the island and how the natives who call themselves 'conchs' see the world. If possible, I walk through cemeteries and take note of the inscriptions on the headstones – especially those who died in the time period I have selected for my story. I record the name, date of birth, date of death and the quotation for the deceased.

In some places, it makes sense to hire a private guide – someone who is knowledgeable of the topics I am there to research. When we went to Auschwitz, I hired a historian to walk through the memorial with us and answer our many questions. He spent the day helping us understand what we were seeing. He also gave me ideas of where to find more information and told us stories that aren't published anywhere. I also found a private guide very helpful when we visited Gettysburg.

I try to leave one whole afternoon free to explore the local library. In some places, local historians hang out there. These folks will talk your ear off once they realize you are interested. In Key West, I met a gentleman who pulled out dozens of dusty tomes filled with clippings that he had collected over the years. They were priceless.

Most libraries have newspaper archives – either in great big bound books or on microfiche. If I'm looking to write about a certain time period, it's helpful to read articles that were written contemporaneously. I focus on the letters to the editor to pick up language, politics and culture. If I have time, I check out the obituaries for the names I recorded at the cemeteries. Oftentimes, there are intriguing stories and characters to be found there. If I don't have time to read everything, I bring lots of change for copies.

When touring national monuments, memorials or museums, it pays to spend time with the caretaker. While touring Fort Jefferson, the park ranger guided me to a set of notebooks kept in the visitors' area where I found a marvelous story about the Fort during World War II. That little story became the basis of a subplot in my novel.

I also spend 'free' time hanging out in bars and restaurants chatting with the locals, listening for the cadence of their speech, enjoying their stories and searching for that special something that makes a place unique and remarkable. I talk with bartenders, waiters, bus and taxi drivers. They know where the 'cool' out of the way places are.

Here are a few tips to remember as you prepare for your trip:

- ✔ Collect resource names, e-mail addresses and telephone numbers.

- ✔ Pick up brochures, business cards and maps.

- ✔ Spend your money for those things you know the least about.

- ✔ Be daring and open to new experiences.

- ✔ Know when to stick to your plan and when to let yourself follow an unexpected lead.

- ✔ Record everything immediately after exposure.

- ✔ Use technology wisely.

- ✔ Don't take more than you can carry.

- ✔ Always wear broken-in, comfortable shoes.

- ✔ Carry a candy bar and a bottle of water.

- ✔ Rest when you are tired.

- ✔ Don't take pictures of charging elephants. Run!

- ✔ Don't leave your purse in the boat.

first published at Scribe & Quill (www.scribequill.com)

Traveling for Research (Part Two) -- Recording What You See -- Low Tech Techniques

by Joyce Faulkner

When I travel for a writing project, I bring along a few tools to help me record, catalog and store the information I collect while on the road. In this piece, I'm going to discuss more traditional techniques, leaving electronic options for another time.

Although I choose a destination based on its attractiveness as a possible location for my novels or for the research facilities available there, I try to keep an eye open for OTHER stories and ideas that could give me material for freelance articles and essays. This means that I collect physical artifacts such as business cards, maps, brochures, schedules, magazines and newspapers. Sometimes these items have no more value than nice mementos, other times they are the source of marketable ideas.

First off, a good digital camera is a must. When entering a town that I plan to write about, I try to take quality photographs of the major features – train stations, market squares, court houses, museums, libraries and the like. Photos of the local gentry are helpful too. I use them to refresh my memory of how people of a given place walk, dress and wear their hair. However, if down the road I decide to write an article about the area, I will have pictures to enhance the value of my work. In any case, I keep a record of picture number, the location, the name of the person in the picture (if recognizable) and whether or not I have a release from that person, the date and the reason I took the picture.

I also carry an old-fashioned blank-paged, spiral-bound, hard cover journal. I buy one for each project while I am in the planning stages and use it to collect hard media during any trips I take and as a scrapbook afterwards. Why am I so particular about it? Well, for one thing, the cheap ones dissolve in my hands like M&Ms on hot concrete. I want the book to fold so that the two backs touch. That way

I have access to the entire area of every page. The binding must be stiff in case I need to take notes standing up. The paper must be thick and of sufficient quality for sketching with either ink or soft pencil.

In addition, I pack a roll of Scotch Tape, a small pair of scissors, a thick rubber band (like the ones that come on heads of cabbage or stalks of celery) and an assortment of pens and pencils. As the book gets thicker, the rubber band keeps it closed and neat as I lug it around. The journal is used for:

- ✔ Sketching scenes, buildings, street maps and people

- ✔ Taking notes and making comments

- ✔ Taping in used tickets, programs, maps, postcards, brochures, menus, business cards, receipts, Xerox copies, letters, etc.

- ✔ Autographs or writing samples

Back in my hotel after my adventures are through, I spend an hour or two organizing the "stuff" I collect. I trim and paste and label everything as required by my internal sense of 'how things should be'. I like to arrange my postings chronologically, for example. Since I may want to paste photographs and printed transcripts of interviews into the book at a later date, I have to 'guesstimate' how many blank pages to leave. So, if I visited the Synagogue in Worms on April 16th at one P.M. and then the Museum at two P.M., I'll cut up the brochures and place the pictures or descriptive text on non-consecutive pages, leaving room for miscellaneous odds and ends. I note down WHY I am saving a particular item and comment on my impressions of the day. Any bright ideas or intriguing questions can be jotted down. I sometimes create long lists of issues to ponder like 'Can you get leprosy from sharing a soup spoon?' or 'Why can't you see a leopard in a dead tree?'

The journal gives me a place to store physical evidence of my daily prowls. By keeping it up to date as I travel, I can evaluate how I'm doing and make decisions about what else I want to learn. I don't have to worry about losing wadded up receipts or wrinkling Xerox copies. Small things like menus may jog my memory at a later date but if they aren't labeled their value is diminished. I'm still kicking myself for throwing away a candy wrapper in Kenya because I can't remember the brand name now.

Once I'm back home, I have at least one box and an index for each project. The index lists all the items that I have collected and in which box they exist. For example, a project file may include the following items: the travel journal, books, magazines, photo negatives and prints, any odd objects that wouldn't fit into the journal, CDs, floppy disks or zip disks and notes about information kept on electronic media. Additionally, I keep the index on my computer so that I can see at a glance everything that I have collected for a given project and know where it is stored.

Organizing information that has been collected does take effort, but there is a satisfaction associated with it too. Many times, small items like train tickets that I kept without appreciating their meaning led me in new directions. This would not have happened if they were wadded up in the bottom of my purse or dropped into the hotel circular file.

first published at Scribe & Quill (www.scribequill.com)

Using Private Guides: A Writer's Eye

by Joyce Faulkner

Travel can be an important resource for writers. Stories and articles gathered through personal visits to famous places are more vivid than those discovered through other research methods. One thing I learned on safari in Africa back in 1999 was that while group tours can be fun, not everyone shares the same interests.

I had long wanted to see Olduvai Gorge which is an archaeological site in northern Tanzania not far from the Serengeti. However, our traveling companions were unimpressed with anthropology in general and Olduvai Gorge in particular. Eager to get to the next stop for lunch, they pushed the guides to cut short this part of the trip. Opting to satisfy the needs of the majority over mine, we were hustled back to the bus and on to the next hotel. Needless to say, I was disappointed and furious.

Since then, I have made it a point to hire private guides when traveling to places that are apt to be once in a lifetime events. The cost isn't that much more than a group tour and the quality of the experience if far more appropriate for the needs of a writer.

For example, to get an overview of the three days of fighting that took place in Gettysburg, Pennsylvania, I found it helpful to hire a ranger to ride with us in my car. For a small fee, he spent a couple of hours driving us around the battlefield describing the events and answering my questions. Our time together was both informative and analytical. It's hard to imagine a guide being able to philosophize about military strategy on that level had we been with a larger group.

In Poland, we found a English speaking guide to take us through Auschwitz. Frankly, this is the best way to experience the memorial for anyone. What happened there is stunning in its simplicity, complex in its technical execution and heartbreakingly profound. Our guide took us to rooms filled with the hair of people who had been gassed sixty years before, explained what we were seeing and then stepped back and allowed us to absorb the reality of it. He told us stories passed on to him by survivors from his own family. He answered my many questions with respectful patience. When I needed to cry, he bowed his head and waited until I found my wits again.

While traveling through Arizona, I found a tour company willing to provide our three person party with a guide. We bounced through the desert in a four-wheel stopping whenever any of us had a question. Our personal wrangler lectured us on the desert flora and fauna, allowed us to pan for garnets and showed us how to shoot potatoes out of a PVC pipe. He taught us about the different cacti, showing us how to get rid of the spines and get to the sweet melon-like flesh. From time to time, he urged us to adjust our hats, take a drink of bottled water and slather ourselves with another layer of sun block. While he explained survival techniques we realized that without him, we city slickers wouldn't be able to survive in this harsh environment.

In Korea, I hired a guide for two days. His fee included his time, his van and the fuel required to visit the sites I had requested and more. He allowed me maximum flexibility to see the things that I wanted to see while offering me options on things he thought I needed to see. He introduced us and translated for us. He read signs and explained customs. He ordered our food at restaurants and took us to the best places for good photographs. At Haeinsa where the writings of Buddha have been stored on wood blocks in a temple high on a hillside, he shared the technical sophistication and the religious significance of the shrine with us. My understanding and appreciation of that beautiful place would have been limited without him.

International travel agencies can put you in touch English speaking guides for foreigners. Although you can often find private tours through the information departments at Memorials, National Parks and Museums, I find it pays to call ahead and make reservations. Phone numbers can be found in tourist guide books, travel agencies and travel web sites. I found my Korean guide through his web site.

first published at Scribe & Quill (www.scribequill.com)

Seek and You Shall Find

by Pat McGrath Avery

A bible verse I've heard since I was a child -- who'd have thought it's such great advice for a writer. It matters not what genre you write, you can improve and embellish your writing if you're a seeker.

How do I define "seeker" for writers? It's simply this. You need an open and inquiring mind. You need excellent observation skills. You need to be curious. If you are always looking around you with open eyes and mind, you will have so much information or topical material that you will never have to ask, "What can I write about?"

Let me give you several examples. First, a fellow author and friend of mine is gifted with an inquiring mind. She's a magnet for story ideas. We recently met in Key West with several other people. As we were sitting around telling stories, she would hear a funny or touching story and immediately tell us "that has to end up in a story someday." You could almost see her brain cataloging the information for future use. She had been in Key West before, taken a tour of the historical sites and struck up conversations with the locals. Everywhere we visited, she related stories or historical facts about the area. All of this while I was being the awe-struck tourist. My mind was filled with visions of sea gulls, pelicans, lush tropical trees and beautiful old homes; hers with a file for future reference. Both of us left filled with creative energy, but I think she left with more story material.

I am the second example. I've written a couple of books on the Korean War. In doing so, I've done a lot of research in libraries, on the Internet, reading books and interviewing veterans. When I started my research, I wondered where I'd find enough veterans to interview. Every fact I learned, most Web sites I visited and almost everyone I interviewed led me to more information or people to contact. I found myself inundated with information -- and all of a sudden, veterans were everywhere. I noticed hats, license plates, bumper stickers -- all about being a veteran. I would stop guys with veteran's hats on and ask them about their experiences. If I was in a parking lot and saw a car with a Korean War license plate, I'd start a conversation.

When I get book orders from individuals, the person is usually a veteran or family of a veteran. I always ask. If he is a veteran, I ask if he'd be willing to let me interview him. There are more stories than I'll ever be able to write.

Another friend writes greeting cards and poetry. She loves people and relationships. She is a great listener and very much in tune with people's emotions. She is able to convert these skills into verse and convey the feelings that so many people can't openly express. Through this, she has made a living writing cards, poetry and has had two books published from her poems.

I've shared these experiences with other writers and found a broad range of responses -- from those who agree with the wealth of opportunity knocking on our doors to those who still can't find anything to write about.

If you fall near or into the latter group, you need to develop these "seeking" skills to become a good writer. You must be observant, be a good listener and develop your brain's database. You need strong organizational skills. If you don't remember things easily, carry a notebook and a camera with you. Take notes and take pictures, then remember to file them properly. I cringe at the number of lost opportunities I've had because I didn't follow simple organizational rules -- lost names and phone numbers, forgotten information, etc.

Luck is what happens when preparation meets opportunity. ~ Elmer G. Letterman

Be prepared. Learn to cross-file information. Much of what we learn can be utilized in and reworked for, various articles, stories or books. Just as you can revise and resell an article, you can re-use a character, a story or pertinent information.

In summary, you need to seek information, listen well, organize your thoughts and notes and store them in your mind's "I'll use this later" file.

The Super Scrapbook: Creating the Project File

by Joyce Faulkner

I am a novelist. Each book I write represents dreams, travel, people and effort. I spend months researching locations and exploring the backgrounds of my characters. I visit automobile dealerships to get a feel for the cars and trucks I use in my books. I wander through memorials and museums and churches. If my hero fought on the island of Iwo Jima, I interview combat marines of that era. If my heroine eats raw octopus, I -- well, maybe I won't go THAT far.

At the conclusion of a project, I have accumulated an incredible amount of 'stuff'. There are notebooks filled with menus, tickets, photos, sketches and receipts. There are magazines, books, transcripts and maps purchased during my quest for background information. The many hours spent in libraries are represented by Xerox copies, handwritten or typed notes and photographs. Interviews include video tapes, mini disks, photographs and transcribed digital files.

On the computer, I build spreadsheets for expenses, plot outlines, editing tools and time lines. I have documents filled with links discovered during Internet searches. I have my contact list. I have a folder for each version of the actual manuscript. All these files are stored on my hard drive, floppies or CDs.

While I'm working, I'd like to tell you that I'm efficient and organized. The fact is that I often work with boxes of chotskies sitting around me. Papers are scattered across my work table and wadded up in the back of my drawers. Unsorted and unlabeled photographs are stacked beside my scanner waiting to be scanned. My notebooks are piled up on the floor beside my bed along with seven or eight tomes waiting to be read. Even more are just out of reach around my recliner where I cozy up to my laptop.

Let's face it, writing's no fun if it's too easy. Clutter raises the bar. Raging about lost files creates the appropriate amount of angst to stimulate the creative process. However, angst aside, as the project approaches its climax, my 'stuff' reaches critical mass and the time to create a project file is nigh.

A 'project file' is a concept borrowed from engineering where a team of people collaborate on designing something BIG like a nuclear power plant. Regardless of rumors about millions of ants being able to build a cathedral, the more folks involved in a job, the greater the chance that something will be over-looked. From the point of view of a single writer, the more elements involved in the project, the more likely one will be left out. The file is a centralized place where everything is kept in order so each piece can be easily found by whoever needs it. It also allows you to make sure that everything required has been addressed.

Although I don't generate an elaborate plan when I write a novel, I do make a list of the steps involved and the things I'll need. I begin with tasks like 'define plot outline', 'prepare character arcs' and 'outline first draft'. As I focus on each action, the catalog expands. Suppose I establish that my main character will be a plastic surgeon. That decision generates additional elements on my agenda -- activities like, 'list books on plastic surgery', 'interview a plastic surgeon', 'explore surgical techniques', etc. As I chase down each one, I learn more and as I learn more, I add more topics to the list. Although it remains fluid until the very end, it becomes the core of my project file.

I suppose that if you are pulling down millions of dollars for each of your books, you can afford to store your project files in cedar or oak file cabinets. I have yet to reach that stage so I use plastic totes and cardboard boxes with lids. Office Max or Staples carry a wide variety of totes. The styles I like have attached lids and rims inside the bins so that you can use hanging files. I suggest that you don't get the larger versions because you can fill them so full that you can't lift them before you know it. For this application, more expensive isn't necessarily better. I choose small and light with stiff sides for correspondence, supplies of things like SASEs, Xeroxed copies of magazine articles, maps, photographs and brochures.

I use cardboard file storage boxes. They are cheaper and lighter for some applications while still being quite sturdy. The less expensive ones come with a flip top, others have a separate lid. You can buy them in multi-unit packages from your local office supply stores or order them on line from places like www.papermart.com or www.staples.com. If you like the idea of file 'drawers', you can get inexpensive, stackable cardboard ones. Acco and Fellowes are two brands that are known for these products.

I like to store things like CDs, Mini-disks and audio tapes in plastic if possible. You can buy so-called 'jewel cases' at the office supply stores or from places like K-Mart and Wal-Mart. Dupont makes a Tyvek window sleeve with a flap if you prefer to store these items in with your hanging files. Another alternative is to use soft plastic sleeves that fit into three-ring binders. With this approach, you can store hundreds of CDs or DVDs in a single book. You can explore your choices at www.sleevetown.com.

A large project may require many boxes. Since over time, I may complete many multi-carton projects, I color code the boxes with round stickers. I organize my files topically rather than chronological or functional. That is, I like to store all the books, CDs, video tapes and maps about Key West in one box as opposed to putting all books in one box and all DVDs in another. That way I'm not rummaging through four or five containers to find what I want when writing about Key West. I label each one with a number, the name of the novel and the topic.

Now here's the thing. I may be anal but I'm also lazy -- a genetic cocktail guaranteed to make the folks around me roll their eyes. The idea of trying to find one little snippet in a mountain of neatly stowed files gives me a headache of gargantuan proportions.

I created the following system so that my husband and I can continue to cohabitate peacefully in the same domicile. I take the original list or 'project plan' and create a database from it -- either on *Access* or *Excel*. Each record has five fields -- Box Number, Topic, Item, Description and Comments. In the description field, I indicate whether the item is a book or DVD or Photograph, etc. In the comments field, I make a note of why this item was collected. This database lives on my computer. It also lives on a 'project file' CD. I sort by box number and print out a sheet listing its contents. This index can be stored in a number of ways. It can be placed into a small envelope and glued to the outside of the box. It can also be kept inside the top of the lid. The key is that it placed so that anyone can be expected to find it.

If while writing about what it's like to fly in an open-cockpit biplane, I become frantic because I can't remember the way the dash is configured in a 1939 WACO, I can console myself by going to the main database on my computer and searching for the word 'PLANE'. From that search, I discover that all information about airplanes is in boxes four and five I do an additional search on the word 'WACO'. The WACO is in box five. Before I go digging through box five, I can scan all the items in it -- things like a video of 'The Great Waldo Pepper', a map of Lock Haven, PA, a book about Pancho Barnes and a series of photographs from the flight we took over Mallory Square at sunset. There's even a photo of the inside of the plane. I rush to retrieve the pictures. There it is. I can see the gauges clearly. Soothed, I sit down and write my scene.

Researching a novel is an enormous investment of money, time and energy. The file helps you evaluate what has been accomplished and what remains to be done. Like a super scrapbook, it gives you a solid image of the places you have visited and the folks you have met. A matchbook from an Indian restaurant in Mannheim Germany might have the telephone number of the cook who said he knew Bono. Not quite as cool as meeting Bono yourself, but it's a start.

first published by *Byline* Magazine

Write, Write, Write!

by Pat McGrath Avery

How many times have you heard those words? Yet how many times have you heard writers complain that they don't write that much because they can't get published? I've attended numerous meetings, conferences and critique sessions where this is at least one person's theme. No matter how many times that person hears it, she just doesn't get the picture.

Sure we all want to write for money -- lots of it -- when successful writers tell you to write, pay your dues and earn recognition, please believe them. They speak from experience.

Lest you think I exempt myself from the writer who doesn't write, I've been there. I'm shy by nature and it's very difficult to submit work and face rejection. To succeed as a writer, you must have the desire and fortitude to seek success. It won't knock on your door. Opportunity may, but you have to take hold and run with it.

I've found the Internet is a great place to get started. There are so many places out there and while most of them pay little or nothing, it's a great place to get experience and to get your name out in front of people.

So, if you're a closet writer who never submits, or just a shy one who finds it difficult, try the easy places first. Get on the Internet, look up sites for writers, book reviewers, etc. The book review is a great way to get started. Many of the sites will tell you that they are constantly looking for reviewers.

Don't think you can't be creative in a book review. I recently read a review that Joyce Faulkner wrote for TheCelebrityCafe.com on <u>The Frugal Book Promoter</u> by Carolyn Howard Johnson. I immediately ordered the book. I had to find out if it's as well written as the review. Some reviews leave me cold with little or no desire to read the book. Others, like Joyce's, make the sale. Try reading a number of reviews.

You'll quickly understand how creativity can sell a book.

Query writer e-zines about articles. These are published by people who are working to build brand recognition, the same as you are. They are interested in any writer who has a story to tell. They want to provide tips to other writers, on writing, marketing, motivation and other subjects of interest. If you can build a portfolio of articles for the Internet, you'll gain confidence, become a better writer, achieve some recognition and make it easier to approach print magazines.

Also approach e-zines in your genre. There are so many of them and they are being read. You will be building a name in your desired field. Get a web site if you don't already have one. Start a blog or a journal. Join in other blogs. There are sites like www.writersweekly.com that post market opportunities. *Funds for Writers* (www.fundsforwriters.com) has two newsletters, based on the size of the market. They list numerous market opportunities. Choose one or both and see what's out there.

Post your work on sites like www.rebeccasreads.com, www.writergazette.com or www.writersmanual.com. I'm only giving you a taste of what's out there. Do a search and you'll understand. Check out the ones that interest you, then submit, submit, submit!

You'll find that if your writing is good, your subjects are timely, your work is error-free, you are professional and you follow directions well, you will get published. Once you do, you will write more and then get published more. The circle of success starts just this way.

Just a note about a couple of the 'ifs' in the last paragraph. Ask any book, magazine or newsletter editor and he will tell you the most frequent causes for a query or manuscript to hit the circular file are submissions that don't follow the guidelines and those full of errors. If you want to be a writer, you must be professional. You may hear stories of a famous author writing a manuscript on napkins, but don't try submitting it. You may write that way, but you don't submit that way.

If you receive a positive response to your query, follow up in a timely manner. Send the requested article or review. Make sure you understand the guidelines and send accordingly. One good thing about Internet submissions -- you don't have to wait as long to get an answer.

If you receive a negative response or no response, review your query letter. Was it professional? Did you follow the guidelines? If you didn't, learn from it. We all make mistakes. A quote I like from an unknown author is: *The only man who makes no mistakes is the man who never does anything.* So stop worrying about past mistakes and keep moving forward.

Keep querying and keep writing. The payoff is great for the morale. You will be inspired to continue writing, you will be more creative and someday, you may make some money.

NETWORKING AND PARTNERSHIPS

Networking for Writers: Harnessing the Power of Teamwork

by Beverly Walton-Porter

Networking with others can be one of your most valuable strategies -- especially if you plan to write full-time and depend on paying assignments to cover your expenses. How do I know this? Simple. Over the past couple of years, I've used networking as a tool to get my words published more and to get paid more for them.

When I quit my traditional job in May of 1997, I jumped into full-time writing with few long-term prospects and zero income. Since then, through networking with other writers and editors to nail down more assignments, I have succeeded in earning more income than from the traditional job I gave up years before.

Not sure how to begin networking? Here are four quick ways to jump-start your networking machine and put the gears in motion that can compel you to obtaining more writing assignments:

1. Join mailing lists, subscribe to free writing e-zines over the Web, study writing Web sites and find newsgroups which welcome and nurture new writers.

2. Build a network of published authors, editors and professional freelance writers and learn from them.

3. Approach like-minded colleagues and build a group that will offer support, honest critique and open exchange of market information or other writing-related assignments.

4. Be ready to give as well as receive information. Make sure to search for freelance job opportunities or calls for articles and post them to your group. Don't sit back and reap all the rewards of someone else's surfing -- if you run across information that doesn't fit your particular genre, but that could be used by another of your group's writers, let them know about it.

Networking is not just for professionals, it's for every level of writer. Teamwork is a powerful concept. Put it to work so that everyone lands consistent assignments.

Anyone Can Network

by Pat McGrath Avery

You've heard it many times before -- networking works! It's true. It's easier for some of us than it is for others, but everyone can learn to do it.

The Internet is the great equalizer. An outgoing person can attend a meeting, a conference or a cocktail party and have great success meeting people. On the other hand, a shy person has to fight to keep from blending into the woodwork. That's where the Internet makes the difference.

I've always found it awkward to be in a room full of people I don't know. It's difficult to walk up to a group of people and join in the conversation. I wilt when I think of the times I've stood around with a group and it seems as if I'm invisible. If you fall into this 'wall flower' category, you understand what I'm talking about.

However, a Google search in the comfort of my home allows me to find a person, send an e-mail and wait for a response without being pushed too far out of my comfort zone. I'm meeting fellow writers, querying editors and asking for research information. When I meet new people, they introduce me to people they've met and a network is born. It's been a great help and a delightful experience.

You can find people in your geographic or writing area. I've found that when I meet a person on line and find out we plan to attend the same writer's conference, I have someone to talk to and I gain courage in reaching out to others.

If I have a question or need information, I can contact the people in my network. If one of them contacts me, I enjoy being helpful in return. Soon you find you're corresponding with several other writers on a regular basis. Everyone wins.

A network contributes to creativity. If you have people who will indulge in brainstorming ideas, your creative mind will be re-energized and you will gain valuable information. If you have a mental block, sharing ideas can work you right out of it.

Local writers and critique groups are great networking tools. Join them and become involved. If you already are, encourage new people to join. The same old group can turn stale. Everyone benefits from new ideas and a fresh point of view.

Keep an open mind. New and experienced writers can learn from each other. Share your energy with others and you will find there's much more energy in you.

Let your neighbors know what you are working on. Become involved in your community. Become friends with the local bookstore folks. Carry your business cards and give them away freely.

Think of yourself as a successful writer. If you are not yet published, envision yourself as a professional and act accordingly. Your frame of mind goes a long way toward determining your reality. Build your reality out of your dream. Think of yourself as a valuable part of any network you're part of -- it's true because every piece of the puzzle is important. That's the beauty of being part of something bigger than yourself.

When You Are Sharing Information

by Joyce Faulkner

Suppose you are interviewing an aging film star who races antique airplanes. Maybe you are writing a thriller and your heroine must conduct an autopsy. Perhaps you are investigating the 1944 Cleveland gas explosion for a short tome on big booms. Most of us aren't acquainted with the details of these subjects. To be able to write about them convincingly, you must collect, understand and assimilate a great deal of unfamiliar information. For that reason, research is the most time consuming and costly part of a writing project.

I have written several historical pieces about the 1940s. I understand the challenges of writing about an era that ended long before I was born. A thousand tiny things are necessary to recreate the world, as it existed during World War Two. People had different appliances than we do now. There were no microwave ovens. Some families had 'iceboxes instead of refrigerators. They wore different clothes. Food was rationed – so were tires. There was no CNN. The populace watched newsreels at movie theaters and listened to radios to learn about current affairs. Everyone smoked. No one drank diet cola. Chasing down these details is quite a job, so now I work with a partner to keep track of the time line and watch for historical inaccuracies.

The only problem is – she lives in St. Louis, I live in Pittsburgh. I'm an engineer and businesswoman at heart. I like an organized approach with a detailed plan and a strict schedule -- especially for big projects like novels. How could we work together without enormous phone bills? How could we avoid the two-day delay (minimum) introduced by using snail mail? Where could we store information that we both could access easily? The answer, of course, was the Internet and a simple tool offered by our friends at Yahoo.

A "Group" is a data repository living on Yahoo's servers accessible from any computer at any time. Although I'll have a lot more to say about security in later columns, you should know that there are risks associated with storing information on line. With the Yahoo product, you can choose who will participate. Curious strangers can be kept at bay, but there is no such thing as a totally secure site. I suggest you evaluate the damage that would come to you if someone hacks Yahoo and steals your material. I wouldn't keep my social security number there, for example, but it's no skin off my nose if a computer nerd in Snowball, Arkansas learns the dimensions of a B-17 from my web site.

The calendar allows the more anal among us to do some simple project management – setting goals, recording achievements and making appointments. You can also arrange for reminders to be sent to your e-mail or that of your partner.

Faxes, scanned articles, spreadsheets, movies or sound bites can be posted to the file storage facility. If you are a "techie", you can pursue the full range of electronic options for interviews – Mini Disk, digital recorders and digital video cameras, for example. I keep copies of completed chapters there as well as outlines and character arcs.

A photo album organizes drawings, photos and maps. I keep pictures of 1940s fashions and World War Two dive-bombers there. A bookmark links the group to pertinent web sites.

A new feature is the database. You can either define your own format or use their templates. Custom designing your own table, you can create a bibliography of books that are on topic or a list of museums, antique stores or locations that you will visit. Although I keep a duplicate of all contacts in my PDA (Personal Data Assistant), it's convenient to keep a Contact List on line so my partner can arrange interviews with people or send out questionnaires.

You can use your e-mail to post messages to the group and you can set it up so that your partner is notified. This function is useful when I want a question to be stored permanently. For example, Mindy once received a note saying, "How do iron lungs work and when did they get invented?" She posted her answers as responses.

The chat room is a practical way to conduct 'two on one' interviews on line in real time. Mindy and I spent several evenings exploring the art of crop dusting with a seasoned ag pilot. Unfortunately, there is no chat log so I recommend using messengers like AOL or MSN to create a text file, which can be saved in the group. Yahoo does have a voice function for verbal conversations, however the static and reverb is intrusive.

To create a group, go to www.yahoo.com and click on "Groups". If you have a Yahoo user name and password, you will be asked to enter them. If not, you will have to go through the registration process. Then you will be presented with a link, "Start a New Group". Yahoo does a good job of walking you through what needs to be done.

The Yahoo Group is not the coolest thing since helium balloons tied into the shape of a fishing pole, but it does the job. It's easy to set up. Two or more people can use it concurrently. The interface is simple and it uses standard language to describe features. Adaptable to the changing needs of an author, it provides sufficient functionality for most writing projects. For those of us who aren't yet bringing in millions, the price is perfect. It's FREE.

first published at *Scribe & Quill* (www.scribequill.com)

WRITING TIPS AND TECHNIQUES

The Complete Writer

Ten BIG Ways to Annoy Book Reviewers

by Joyce Faulkner

I review four or five books a month. I read more but when I can't find anything nice to say I prefer to say nothing. It's not that I'm all that hard-nosed. I have a heart despite what others might say about me. However, there are a few things that set my teeth on edge. In the interest of fairness, I'm willing to share them with authors who can either avoid sending their books to me or avoid some of the general issues that make me nuts.

1. Avoid extraneous descriptions. If the color of a character's eyes has nothing to do with the plot, please spare me. Every word should count toward the point you are making. Endless discourse about waves on the sand better mean something in the course of your story or I'll ding you on it.

2. Minimize passive voice. I'm not adverse to a sentence here or there, but if every other verb is passive I get bored. If it turns into pages of passivity, I'm unlikely to review your book -- and if I do, I'm liable to be cranky.

3. Limit the long sentences and academic snootiness. I have advanced degrees too. Trying to impress me doesn't impress me. Showing off turns me off.

4. Don't repeat yourself. The old business adage of 'tell them what you are going to tell them, tell them and then tell them what you told them' might work for the lowest common denominator, but I find it insulting and a waste of space.

5. Don't preach. I can handle it in an article, but it's exhausting when it goes over two thousand words. At one hundred pages, it's excruciating.

6. Know what you are talking about. If I spot obvious mistakes or if your premise has logical flaws, I'll start fact checking. Reviews of books where I've found errors include discourses

on my incredulity and your credibility.

7. <u>Minimize the he/she saids</u>. Most of the time, I know who's speaking from the sense of the sentence or the sequence. If I can't tell, then your dialog needs help anyway.

8. <u>Don't use the same word twice in one paragraph</u>. That's enough to annoy me. The same word twice in one sentence will drive me right over the edge. Let's face it, that's why God gave us Thesauruses.

9. <u>Get to the point</u>. A book that circles a point is almost as bad as a pointless book. Don't waste my time.

10. <u>Know when to stop</u>. If you can say it in two hundred pages, don't stretch it out to four hundred pages. I can recognize filler at five hundred paces.

first published at *Scribe & Quill* (www.scribequill.com)

Editing Techniques Using Microsoft Word Functions

by Joyce Faulkner

I don't understand this right brain/left brain controversy. Perhaps that's because I'm either an engineer who writes, or a writer who engineers. No matter how you slice it, creativity is a technical endeavor. Great prose doesn't 'just happen' -- it is created during the editing process.

Today helpful editing tools are built right into Microsoft Word, a commonly used computer program available for both PCs and Macs. Most people rely on the spell checker and the ability to easily reformat text. Many are familiar with the "cut and paste" function. However, few writers use the SPELLING AND GRAMMAR routine.

Found under TOOLS on the main menu, SPELLING AND GRAMMAR runs like spell checker. It points out potential grammatical errors and gives you the opportunity to make corrections as the program scans your text. In the end, "Readability Statistics" are calculated and published. (If you don't see the function, it's possible that your installation of Word has it disabled. Go to Tools, Options, Spelling & Grammar Tab and enable 'Show Readability Statistics'.)

The statistics consist of three main categories -- counts, averages and readability. Counts give you the number of words, characters, paragraphs and sentences in your file. Averages give sentences per paragraph, words per sentence and characters per word. Readability gives you the percentage of passive sentences, Flesch reading ease score and the Flesch-Kincaid grade level.

The first handy tool in the 'Readability Statistics' is the percentage of passive sentences. Editors have long implored writers to minimize their passive sentences -- but what is the proper percentage? Personally, I like to keep passive sentences in the one percent range for my action novels. I don't mind going up to two or four percent for short stories and articles, but more six percent makes me a little insane.

For example, when I first wrote this article and ran the readability statistics, it came out eight percent passive sentences -- not acceptable to me for this audience. I went back and transformed passive sentences into active ones. When I finished, the number was four percent -- three passive out of seventy-two sentences.

Rudolph Flesch developed the Flesch reading ease score in the 1940s based on the physiology of human comprehension. It works like this: Your brain makes tentative decisions about what words mean as your eye scans the passage. When you get to a conclusive punctuation mark, you pause and assess what you have absorbed so far before arriving at a final meaning of all the words put together.

The longer the sentence, the more ideas your mind has to collect, store and evaluate. That means you have to concentrate more. On top of that, longer words send more signals to your brain. 'Love' is short and sweet and easy to understand. 'Affectionate' has more letters and more syllables to absorb and interpret. Thus, longer words in longer sentences make you work harder than shorter words in shorter sentences.

The Flesch reading ease score rates text on a one hundred point scale. Measuring the average sentence length and the average word length, it puts the results into a formula. The higher the score, the easier it is to read your work. According to Rudolph Flesch, plain English has a score between sixty and seventy. Below forty is considered difficult to read. Comics rank above ninety. *Reader's Digest* comes in around sixty-five. The *Wall Street Journal* rates a forty-three. The Internal Revenue Tax Code is minus six.

So now, you have a meaningful guideline for establishing the level of your work. Before you begin an article, assess the reading level the editors want to maintain by reviewing past issues or simply asking. Then monitor the level of your manuscript by running the SPELLING AND GRAMMAR algorithm as you write. If your score is lower than the goal, break long sentences into shorter ones. Replace complex words with simple ones. If your score is higher than the goal, use a thesaurus to find alternate expressions. Add subordinate clauses to your sentences. After making your edits, re-check your Flesch score and adjust again as necessary.

For example, I write thrillers for a general audience. I want my readers to have fun. Although the plots are complex, the eye should literally fly over the page. I try to keep my Flesch scores between eighty and ninety. On the other hand when I write for *Scribe & Quill*, I am communicating with an educated audience interested in a specific topic. That means I need a lower Flesch score. However, this is not a text book. Subscribers of e-mail newsletters expect something entertaining. Therefore, I aim for a range between sixty and seventy. This particular piece came in at sixty.

Another way to control manuscript readability is by using the Flesch-Kinkaid algorithm. It rates text at the U.S. grade school level. For example, a score of 4.0 means that a fourth grader can understand the passage. The 1992 Adult Literacy Survey indicated almost half of American adults read at or below the eighth grade level. Therefore, a rating of 8.0 is a reasonable starting point for general audiences. Then you can adjust up or down as required. The ranking of this article is 8.0.

Finding the right level heightens acceptance. Many great stories aren't widely read. How many high school seniors would select <u>Moby Dick</u> or <u>The Scarlet Letter</u> on their own? On the other hand, comic books remain popular, generation after generation. As Eileen Dryer said at the Pike's Peak Writer's Conference, "If you intend to sell what you write, you are in show business." That means setting your language goals to fit the comprehension requirements of your target audience. In the olden days, calculating these scores on a document of any size was tedious. Microsoft Word simplified the process and made it easy for authors to edit their work.

first published at *Scribe & Quill* (www.scribequill.com)

Spell Checker -- a Blessing and a Curse

by Joyce Faulkner

Once upon a time in a land far, far away, I decided to write a word processor from scratch using a language called BASIC. This was back when I owned a tiny sixteen bit computer where you saved your stuff on cassette tapes. Don't ask me why I thought this might be a good idea. Perhaps it was because I didn't know how to cook and I'd already seen all the reruns of 'I Love Lucy'.

The experience left me with a great appreciation for Microsoft Word, Corel WordPerfect, Sun Star Writer and Lotus WordPro. These big bad programs provide writers with functionality way beyond that of my simple design so many years ago. They broaden our ability to create polished manuscripts and reduce the amount of time it takes to do individual projects.

One of the most useful tasks provided by these word processors is spell checker. When I was introduced to the concept in the early 1980s, it seemed truly miraculous. Imagine having a machine scan a document and figure out if a particular word is misspelled. I was enchanted.

However, now that the honeymoon is over, my expectations are higher. What was once luxury is now standard operating practice. I have grown older -- and spell checkers are as fallible as I am, unfortunately. In fact, I had a close encounter of the unpleasant kind with my word processor last month when I was writing an article for *Scribe & Quill*. While trying to be erudite and clever, I used a couple of words that I didn't know I didn't know how to spell -- 'onomatopoeia' and 'prestidigitator'.

I ran Microsoft Word's 'Spelling and Grammar Checker'. Although it caught many problems, it didn't highlight those two words. When the article was published, *Scribe & Quill*'s spell checker didn't catch them either. The *Scribe & Quill* audience caught them though. No hiding anything from smart people.

Mortified, I set to work to figure out what was wrong. Microsoft Word XP comes with the Standard American English Dictionary. It contains most common words, but might not include proper names, technical terms, acronyms and so on. Sometimes the main dictionary doesn't incorporate alternate forms of a word -- like 'color' and 'colour', for example. It's no big deal -- you can add the different versions to the custom dictionary through the 'Spelling and Grammar' tool.

Another approach for this problem is what's called an 'exclude' dictionary. It contains words that the main dictionary recognizes as being correct, but that you want questioned for specific projects. For example, the word 'seal' is included in the main dictionary. Maybe you want to name a main character 'Seele' -- and you want to make sure that throughout the story, Word flags the use of 'seal'. Using an exclude dictionary also permits you to specify preferred spellings. Instructions for this technique appear in the Microsoft Word Help feature.

Once in a while, misspellings or 'mistypings' accidentally create words that exist in the main dictionary. For example, 'barest' is a finger-stutter away from 'breast'. These errors are hard to see since the program doesn't flag them. If the mistake changes the structure of the sentence, the grammar checker might catch it -- but most of the time, you have to find it by visual inspection. One solution is to let your document set for a day or two before reviewing it. Another is to ask a friend to look at it.

The most difficult situation is when a word does not appear in the main dictionary at all. This happens when the writer is dealing with a specialized vocabulary -- like onomatopoeia or prestidigitator, for example. Third party vendors offer extensive word lists for medical, biblical, scientific and other technical topics. During installation or at any time afterwards, you can choose whether Word should use all or some of these products instead of or in conjunction with the main dictionary.

Another way to include unusual words is to create a custom dictionary. This may be the best approach for those of you working in fantasy. If you are constructing a piece where people, places and things have odd names or where your characters speak non-standard languages, you may find this is the best way to go. It's unlikely that 'Klaatu, Barata, Nikto' appear in the Standard American English Dictionary.

If your project requires unusual capitalizations or acronyms, you can add these items to existing custom dictionaries through the 'Spelling and Grammar Checker'. This is a nice feature in that it isn't intrusive to your work flow. You can find instructions for creating or modifying a custom directory in the Help menu.

Building these custom dictionaries is worthwhile because Microsoft makes them available to other Office products such as FrontPage, PowerPoint, Publisher and Excel as well as Word. They are useful for making sure that odd spellings are consistent when using a variety of tools and you can switch them on or off as required for the project at hand.

For those of you working on multi-lingual projects, foreign language dictionaries included with Microsoft Word are Arabic, Chinese, Danish, Dutch, Finnish, French, German, Greek, Hebrew, Italian, Japanese, Korean, Norwegian, Polish, Portuguese, Russian, Spanish, Swedish and Thai. You can also select specialized keyboarding and the ability to spell check in these languages.

I had no idea how important this function was until I spent a month in Germany. To my surprise, the computers in an Internet Café in Mannheim didn't use standard QWERTY keyboards. After sending my friends a series of unintelligible e-mails, I resorted to the time honored 'hunt and peck' system. For a touch typist, the results were inefficient and hilarious.

If working in English is difficult on a word processor set up for German, imagine how difficult it is to work in Japanese or Korean on programs configured for English. For instructions on how to reconfigure the keyboard or select spell-check dictionaries for other languages, look at the on line help functions

This short review of Microsoft Word's spell checking capabilities increased my regard for the power of this program. However, it's not the magic bullet that I'd hoped to find. The problem isn't technological but human -- if you don't know how to spell a word in the first place, how are you going to find it in a dictionary or thesaurus?

Word can help you with this dilemma if your initial effort comes within a stone's throw of the correct spelling and if the word is included in the database to begin with. However, it seems that no matter how complete a dictionary may be, English is a living language. New words are coined all the time.

Automatic spell checkers are wonderful tools -- but they work in conjunction with humans. Their effectiveness is dependent upon the underlying dictionaries, which must be kept up to date and pertinent. For the time being, writers must continue working with keen-eyed editors and proofreaders to ensure clean copy ready for publication. Darn. I really wanted to believe in Santa Claus.

first published at *Scribe & Quill* (www.scribequill.com)

I'm Your Reader: Ten Things I Hate

by Joyce Faulkner

I'm a reader. I buy LOTS of books. I read even more. I like both fiction and nonfiction. I write reviews. I trade paperbacks with other folks. I recommend them to my friends. In fact, I'm your prime audience – the fish that can bring other fish to your hook. The problem is, I don't really know what I like -- but I do know what I hate.

1. I hate to be bored. In fact, if you bore me, you've lost me -- and if you lose me, I'm pretty loose-lipped about it. Things that bore me include preaching, sports without a point, rambling and long, convoluted sentences. I don't care much for phony dialects either although you can win me over if the story starts right away. More than a sentence or two of narrative puts me to sleep and my eyes glaze over when you describe things in flowery detail.

2. I hate when you don't get to the point right away. You can tease me if you're writing a novel, but don't even think about it in nonfiction. I'm impatient by nature and won't give you but a page or two before I put down your book for good. This is a corollary to writing for the web where I'll give you about six seconds to capture my attention and maybe thirty seconds to get to the meat of your discourse.

3. I hate lots of adjectives in one sentence. One or two, I'll give you. Three you are beginning to get on my nerves. More than that is an unforgivable lapse in good judgment and although I won't put down your book on that account, I'll make nasty comments about it to my friends.

4. I hate lots of adverbs. When I read Jon Katzenbach's <u>Hart's War,</u> I found a sentence that had four 'ly' adverbs in it and declared Katzenbach the all time champion over-user of adverbs. I was sure it was a record that would stand. Then, just the other day, a new writer sent me his book. The very first sentence had FIVE 'ly' adverbs! Since the next sentence was a half page long, I closed the file and sent it back

to him with a non-committal 'nice' in the subject line of my e-mail.

5. I hate when you use expressions over and over throughout your manuscript. It raises the hairs on the back of my neck if you use the same word twice in one paragraph. With all the dictionaries and thesauruses in the world, it seems odd that a writer can't come up with new and different ways to say things. Like the adjective and adverb thing, it's distracting. I find myself keeping score rather than reading your book. For example, I reviewed a novel excerpt where the author used "distinctly" three times in the first paragraph, six times in the first page and twenty-two times in the first chapter. What was the piece about? I don't know. I was too busy counting.

6. I hate when words are misused. I know how hard it is to catch those little slips. I had a piece of writing where I used the word 'racked' instead of 'wracked'. Spell-check can't find mistakes like that. I rewrote that document five times and never noticed it. My husband missed it. A friend did a line by line check and didn't spot it. It wasn't until I saw the printed page that it popped out at me. Even so, as a reader, it's annoying to come across 'there' instead of 'their' or 'horse' instead of 'hoarse'. Whether your characters 'peak' or 'peek' can leave your readers wondering what you mean.

7. I hate when you let language interfere with the story. Oh I know that writers love playing with words and phrases. It's great fun to work in alliteration or onomatopoeia from time to time, but having your character call someone a 'sweet, sultry, solipsistic slut' or have him buzz like a bee is going too far.

8. I loathe redundancy. I'm only willing to give you so much time. In nonfiction, I'll accept repetition for emphasis. The old, 'Tell them what you are going to tell them, tell them and then tell them what you told them' maxim works for technical information but becomes annoying when the material is simple. In fiction, the axiom is 'Mention an item three times if you want a reader to remember it.' That may be true, but use the technique with care. It sometimes comes off as a mistake instead of an experimental technique to build suspense.

9. Don't promise me one thing and deliver another. The best way to make sure I never buy another one of your books is to surprise me in

an unacceptable way. For example, if you sell me a horror story that turns out to be a romance, I'll be disappointed. Fantasy and erotica are different. If I'm doing research on the criminal justice system, I don't want to get to the end of the piece and find out I've been reading fiction. I know what I'm getting when I read Anne Rule or Stephen King or Nelson DeMille. Don't play with me and pretend to be something you aren't.

10. I hate when an author's personal opinions intrude on the story. That's not to say that I don't appreciate that most material has a perspective or voice. However, I don't like to have it rubbed in my face. For example, Aphrodite Jones is an excellent investigative journalist. Her book <u>Red Zone</u> about the San Francisco dog mauling case is well-researched and readable. It's clear that while Robert Noel and Marjorie Knoller fascinate Ms. Jones, they also disgust her. The defendants' words and actions show them for what they are, but the author lingered over Marjorie's appearance. As I read, I realized that intrusion of self into the narrative left me thinking ill of Ms. Jones rather than Marjorie Knoller and ultimately lowered my opinion of the overall piece.

As a reader, I'm capricious and unforgiving. As writers, you can lure me in so many ways. Don't let me slip off the hook before you can reel me in.

first published by *Scribe & Quill* (www.scribequill.com)

MOVING ON

Six Easy Steps To Launching Your Own E-zine

by Beverly Walton-Porter

So, everyone on the 'Net has an e-zine -- except you, right? And you aim to have the coolest e-zine out there, but you don't know how to get there, or what road to take.

Worry no more -- here you'll learn six quick and easy steps for setting up your own e-zine. And you'll be up and running with the avant garde techno-publishing pack in no time at all -- guaranteed!

'Zine Master Or Mistress: Will You Have What It Takes?

The most important factor in an e-zine is the big "C" -- content. Anyone who wants to publish an e-zine should do the following:

- ✔ provide accurate, interesting, well-edited content (original, if possible)

- ✔ keep a regular schedule for distribution

- ✔ pay your writers if you are able to do so and pay them in a timely manner

- ✔ promote your magazine and its contents

Seems like a pretty tall order to fill? Well, you're right. But with all the sweat and tears and clumps of hair you'll be pulling out during the birthing stages of your 'zine, you'll also come to know a strange sense of accomplishment -- a Zen-like serenity. Or, perhaps when it's all over, you'll just pump your fists in the air and wail, "Heck yeah -- I DID it!" Yes, you'll do it, all right. I'll show you how.

1. Are You Up To The Challenge?

Before you rev up your keyboard and get down to business, 'zine style, you'll need to ask yourself some hard questions -- and hope you come up with the right answers! The obvious first question is: why do you want to throw yourself into the e-zine publishing arena?

Here's where reality sets in, my friends. E-zines are fun in a lot of ways -- not to mention the instant recognition you'll get from family, friends and Internet acquaintances.

But do you really know **why** you're starting up the e-zine in the first place? Is it just a novel idea, or do you really think there's a reader niche to fill? Tricky questions, but in order to be a successful 'zine publisher, you'll need to answer them.

Once you've determined that you're a prime candidate for launching your own e-zine, then comes the next set of questions you'll need to cover. Will you publish your 'zine every week, two weeks or every month? Or will you opt for a quarterly 'zine, packed with more information in a sort of deluxe issue?

Remembering that content is king of the e-zine world, consider the main focus of your 'zine -- whether it's covering the club scene, catering to the techie crowd or bonding with those who share your hobbies and interests, such as indie films or alternative music. Depending on your decided-upon pub schedule, will you have more than enough fresh and useful content to sustain your 'zine for the long haul?

If the answers to all these questions are "yes," then you're ready for stage two.

2. Do You Know Your Readers?

Now that you're sure you're ready, willing and able to start your own 'zine, you'll need to answer a major question before you shoot out of the gate and head straight ahead into reader territory. In fact, you'd better know the inhabitants of that territory -- and know them well. After all, what good is a 'zine without readers, after all?

First and foremost, who ARE your readers? What subjects will you cover in your 'zine? Will your 'zine be of the general, mainstream Gen-X variety, or are you going for more specific niches? Before you dip your paws into the publishing pond, you'd better know what creatures are gonna' flock to your end of the cove.

Going back to the final point in step one above, you'll need to make sure you've got more than enough resources to draw upon to satisfy their ravenous cravings on a weekly, bi-weekly or monthly basis.

3. Finding Your Readers

To focus in on who your readers are and how to find them, use the classic questions from journalism: who, what, where, when, why and how. How old are your readers and of what sex? You might want to take a scratch piece of paper and work up a basic profile of your ideal reader as you go through the sections below. This will keep you focused on your readership goal.

Do you plan to deliver information to readers only in your country of origin, or are you planning on a global voice for your publication? Will you deliver the goods by e-mail and post your 'zine on the Web, too?

Once you've honed in on who your typical reader is, you'll need to find out how to tap into that well of readership. How do you do this? By finding out where your potential readers are hanging out, what other 'zines they're reading or Web sites they're frequenting.

Since you should already have a grasp on who your readers are, along with a basic profile of sorts, it's time to surf in search of your soon-to-be loyal following.

Consider their aptitude level (Are you writing to the student level, or to the academic crowd? Are you catering to professionals or blue collar workers in your age group?) Depending on your answers, you'll be able to develop a clear idea of where your potential group hangs out -- then it's time to search and employ their readership!

Next in line comes the crucial "why" question. Why will these people flock to your publication? Why are they such a unique crowd and how are you gonna give them the info or entertainment fix they're craving? Make a list of items you think they will expect in your 'zine and how you plan to keep it fresh.

Another all-important question to ask is where you're going to find your readership. We've already touched up this briefly, but you need to map out a plan for not only where to gain your first wave of readership, but where is the best place to advertise to bring in a steady stream for the months and years ahead.

Link exchanges work well -- but only if you exchange links with Web sites that cater to the crowd you're targeting. Be very selective before you ask if you can exchange links with a Web site -- how many visitors, or page hits per day, is that Web site getting? Opt for sites that are bringing in the traffic.

You might also place ads in print 'zines that have a large group of readers who are on line often. Be sure to add a .sig, or signature line, to all your outgoing e-mail messages, too. Let people know you're the publisher of your newly founded 'zine.

Also, find out what mailing lists or newsgroups are attracting your potential readers and when the prime time they're visiting is. If you're targeting the gaming crowd, find out the highest ranked gaming centers where they'll likely be congregating. In other words, if you go there and beckon them in a tactful, non-"spam" way, they will come.

Finally, you'll need to determine how you are similar to your readers. This might mean there's a geographical similarity or, perhaps, a similarity in sports, hobbies, philosophies or religious beliefs. The more similarity that exists, the better.

4. Getting Up and Running

There's no real secret to getting the e-zine itself up and running. In fact, most 'zines are nothing more than text-based mailings. You can find some Web-based 'zines with templates out in cyberspace, such as at www.zinezone.com, but many quality e-zines are simply text-based.

To successfully reach as many readers as you can, start out with a plain, text-based document sent via e-mail. For now, forget the fancy stuff and forgo the HTML-enhanced mailings. Remember, "C" for content, is the main element of a successful 'zine.

For best success, e-zine experts recommend using a basic text editor to create your 'zine. A text editor is nothing more than a program you use to compose your text file. Most people use Windows, so Notepad will do, or you can create a text document in Word or WordPerfect, as well. If, for some reason, you don't have a text editor -- which most people do -- then there are plenty of free text editors for download on the 'Net.

Once you have a text editor handy, now it's time to begin composing your e-zine. While you're filling your new 'zine with wonderful or cutting-edge content, be sure to observe these hard and fast rules to give your publication the most professional look possible:

✔ Design a nameplate. Simply put, the nameplate is the intro or "opener" for your 'zine. In the nameplate, you'll list your 'zine's title, a one-sentence tagline which captures the essence of your 'zine, the date and the volume and issue of the 'zine. Here is an example:

****

Quoth the Quill ~~ The 'zine for writers of all genres

Vol. 2, Issue 4 September 1999

****

✔ Include a masthead. This is where you'll list important details about your 'zine, such as contact information of the publisher, copyright notices, information on how to subscribe or unsubscribe and advertising details.

✔ Use a table of contents. An example of this might be:

> Editor's Corner
>
> Reader Feedback
>
> WebWatch Column: "Raves on the Web"
>
> Feature Article: "Tracking the Elusive Web Maven"
>
> Monthly News & Reviews

Whatever you include in your 'zine, be sure readers know the order of the content and the title of each article or feature.

✔ Don't type in ALL CAPS. It's hard on the eyes -- and it's the equivalent to SCREAMING. Come into your recipients' e-mail boxes like a lamb, not a lion.

✔ Since you'll be using a text-based format, rather than a HTML-based format, if you need to emphasize a word, or make a part of your 'zine stand out from the rest, then use asterisks (*) to make your **point**.

✔ Forget using word wrap. Make a hard line break at the end of each sentence by pressing the "enter" key.

✔ Instead of using the "tab" key, which may not have the same setting on your system as someone else's, simply use the space bar if you need to indent paragraphs.

✔ To avoid unnecessary extra spaces between sentences or paragraphs, end typewritten lines at sixty-five characters. If you're unsure about how long (and this includes letters AND spaces) that is, at the top of your page template, type sixty-five "x's" – then follow that example, making sure not to allow your typed sentences to go past the final "x."

✔ If you plan to add any kind of ASCII art in your 'zine, make sure your works of art will be displayed the same on your machine, as it is on your recipient's machine. For most purposes. ASCII art is cute and artistic, but it might be best left out of your 'zine.

5. Generating Consistent Content

You're now officially a publisher of an e-zine, but can you stretch yourself thin enough to be sole reporter for your 'zine? Of course not. The next question is, how do you find that all-important "C," or content, for your publication?

Some items in your 'zine, such as an "editor's corner" will obviously be written by you. Then you can openly recruit friends or acquaintances who are interested in contributing to the 'zine in the way of columns or feature articles. In the beginning, you may be short of cash and unable to pay your writers -- but if at all possible, make an effort to do so, as soon as advertising funds are available.

Seeing your name on a masthead will only go so far and professional writers who make a living by researching or writing articles, generally require some sort of payment for their efforts.

On occasion, you will be able to locate an interesting article that's been printed once before and after contacting the author, you may be able to run the article at no additional charge. Whatever you do, don't use anyone's articles or columns without receiving permission first!

As for other content, interviews are always a winner with readers. They like to meet movers and shakers and they like the personal edge to an interview article. Also, you might open a reader's forum, which allows readers to vent their concerns or post their questions in a Q & A monthly column.

If you're still hard up for content, some 'zine sites offer free articles for the taking. One such site is at www.e-zinez.com.

6. Distributing Your 'Zine

It's already been mentioned that your 'zine will be distributed via e-mail, but how do you do that, you ask? You can do it the easy way, or the hard way.

Initially, you might think it's best to just manage the list yourself by manually adding a group mailing list to your e-mail software. This means you'll be responsible for personally answering every subscribe/unsubscribe request that lands in your e-mail box.

Unfortunately this can quickly become the hard way when your 'zine subscriber list grows. You'll find yourself spending more and more time just trying to keep up with list management tasks.

On the other hand, the easy way to set up your mailing list is to use a mailing list server. There are many of these servers on the 'Net, but a couple of the most popular include:

http://www.topica.com

http://www.groups.yahoo.com

These mailing list servers make it easier on you once your list grows. Many of them also offer extra perks and features, such as group chat rooms, polling, databases and statistic reports, so you can gauge

162

what countries or domains your subscribers are coming from and how they found your 'zine.

Final Words on 'Zine Publishing

You can never do enough research for your 'zine. In fact, you'll need to surf the 'Net regularly to find the most up-to-date information on what's happening in the world of 'zines and what 'Netizens want most in their 'zines.

For everything you need to know about getting your 'zine up and running, to what's being published and by whom, check out these excellent sites regularly:

http://www.ezineseek.com/

http://ezine-tips.com/

http://bestezines.com/

http://www.zinebook.com/

http://www.e-zinez.com

http://www.ezine-news.com

Launching your own e-zine involves more than just technical details -- it's also about finding your reader niche, courting and keeping those readers and finally, delivering the content and product your readers expect.

With research and planning, you can stake your claim on the 'Net with a 'zine that will draw'em in -- and keep'em coming back -- month after month and issue after issue!

Self Publishing

by Pat McGrath Avery

You have a manuscript and a box of rejection slips. Maybe you have that manuscript and do not want to share your creative authority. Maybe you just want to do a family history and give it to everyone you know. In any case, you think you have a good book and you want to get it out there. This book has been about writing that book. Now we're going to take it a step further and talk about self-publishing your finished product.

Let's take the time to look at the pros and cons of becoming a self publisher.

You will find there are a multitude of good books out there that tell you how to proceed. We are not going to try and give you the whole process in a few pages. What we want you to do is gain a realistic picture of what your options are. We have included a sample list of those books at the end of this article.

There are several possibilities: POD (print on demand) where you are the publisher, POD companies that become your publisher, PQN (print quantity needed) book printers where you are the publisher, traditional book manufacturers that do small-to-large book runs and subsidy presses that do all the work for you.

There is a commonality in all of these options. You and you alone, will be responsible for layout, editing and proofreading. Some companies will offer these services for extra money, but it is not included in the basic fee. I will talk more about that later.

POD (print on demand) -- This has become the ideal way for many people who plan on selling just a few books. There is an up-front fee starting in the $400 to $500 range. That includes the set up cost and in some cases, a few copies of the book. It does not include any of the editing or proofing services listed above. You pay the fee, send in your manuscript as a camera ready file and they turn it into a book.

PROS

✔ You print copies only as you need them. You never have to worry about warehousing a bunch of books.

✔ The cost is not prohibitive for most people. It is almost always under $1,000 to get started.

✔ The quality of the paper and cover is usually good. The overall quality of the book will depend on what you send them.

✔ Most POD companies will list your book in all their publications and with a distributor. You will not have to take care of those details. You can spend your time marketing the book.

CONS

✗ The company does nothing to assure the quality of your work. You are completely responsible for editing, proofreading and cover design. You can pay extra to have these services performed for you, but that adds to the cost. If you do not have proper margins, it will show up in the final copy. If you have errors, they will show up. This is a very important issue and you need to determine how you will deal with it. If you want quality, you will have to pay for these services!

✗ Many companies will issue the book under their ISBN and they will then be listed as the official publisher. Their name appears on the book. Book stores and libraries recognize those names immediately. If you want to become a publishing company and buy a block of ISBNs, you can avoid this issue.

✗ Many bookstores and libraries will not carry or buy POD books. You need to be aware of this if you are pursuing traditional book markets. If you are planning on selling on your web site or at presentations you give, then it will not matter.

✗ Most POD books have very low sales volume. There is no sales support from the publisher. Marketing is left up to you, the author. Many people do not really want to sell books, they just want to have a book in print. That has skewed the numbers. When you see statistics that state POD books average about one hundred copies sold, keep in mind that people publish their books for a variety of reasons.

PQN (print quantity needed) -- This is a good way to print books if you want to do a small run and spend minimal money. You can secure bids on as few as one hundred copies from most companies.

PROS

✔ You become the publisher. You are using your own ISBN and you own the book. This is both a pro and a con because it makes you responsible for all the legal listings and getting set up with a distributor.

✔ The cost per book is usually lower than POD if you figure in initial set up costs.

✔ You can easily go back for reprints if you sell all your copies.

✔ Most companies have web sites where they will list your book.

CONS

✗ You have limited sizes available from many of the companies. Most start with one hundred copies, whereas with POD, you can buy one copy at a time.

✗ You have to become a publisher to effectively sell your books.

✗ Per copy cost is higher in small runs than in large runs.

Traditional Book Manufacturers -- These are the companies that manufacture large orders of books.

PROS

✔ They usually produce high quality books.

CONS

✗ They are expensive. Usually you will need to run one thousand or more copies and this is expensive if you do not have a good marketing plan in place.

✗ You have to find some place to store these books. They take up a lot of space.

✗ You can end up with a great number of books on your hands that you no longer want.

✗ There are no editing or proofreading services provided.

Subsidy Printers -- These companies ask you to pay them for publishing your book. It is not just the cost of printing. It is the way they make their profits. It is usually more expensive than POD. You typically pay a large sum of money and get five hundred to a thousand books in return.

PROS

✔ It is a way to get your book published.

CONS

✗ It is very expensive.

✗ Subsidy publishers are well-known but not well-loved within the industry. You will have a hard time getting your book in stores.

✗ There are no editing or proofreading services provided.

Setting Up Your Own Publishing Company

Now that we have looked at the opportunities, you may still want to publish on your own. Please be aware that the whole marketing load will fall on your shoulders. While it is a fact in today's world that all authors need to promote themselves, it will be more critical for you to do so.

If we still have not discouraged you, then let's look at what is needed to get started. Let's assume that you have your manuscript in process or completed.

To become a publisher, you will need to set up your own publishing company. You will need to do a number of business-related functions.

- ✔ Select a name and register it with your state. Before you do this, you need to research the name and make sure it is not being used. You can pay an attorney to have this done for you and then you will be sure no one else is using that name. Or you can do a reasonable search on your own. You can search directories of publishers in your library. You can search through companies like www.amazon.com and www.bn.com. You can try to secure a domain and see if that name is taken. Take the time to do the research. If you end up with a name that someone else is using, you will be setting yourself up for confusion from distributors, suppliers and customers.

- ✔ Secure any licenses needed. Check with your city about a business license. You may need to register at the county and state level, too. In some states, once you file a fictitious name, you do not need to register it in any other way. To be sure, check your state's requirements.

- ✔ You will need to secure a state sales tax number. If you are incorporating, you will need a Federal ID number known as an EIN. If you are setting up as a sole proprietorship or partnership, your business number will be your social security number.

168

✔ You must buy a set of ISBNs from RR Bowker. These are the folks who keep track of all the books in print and publish the list, <u>Books in Print</u>. You can access them through the Internet at www.bowker.com. There is a cost for this. At present, to register as a publisher for ten numbers, the fee is $19.95. Then it costs $225 to buy the ten numbers. You cannot buy less than ten numbers at a time.

✔ Send for copyright forms through the Library of Congress. Check www.loc.gov. Click on the Publishers section. There you will find information you need on copyright, the PCN (preassigned control number) for library cataloging and the CIP (cataloging in publication) record, bibliographic information prepared by the Library of Congress.

✔ Secure your domain name and build a web site. You will need an Internet presence even if you do not want to sell books from your site. An informational site is fine. You need to be available to people who search for information about you, your company and your books.

Once you have your business set up, you will need to work on your book.

✔ Set a publication date. Give yourself at least six months to get everything done. You need to secure reviews and testimonials to help sell your book.

✔ Assign an ISBN number and register your book with Bowker. You will need to fill out an ABI (Advanced Book Information) to have your book registered in <u>Books in Print.</u> Order a bar code.

✔ Design both your front and back cover. On the back cover, you need to sell your book. Solicit testimonials from experts in the field. If you have money, get help here. People do judge a book by its cover. They are attracted to a front cover and then typically check out the back cover. Both need to be marketing tools for you.

✔ Do book layout and design. When your manuscript is completed, you will be responsible for this. If you are not an expert at the computer, consider hiring someone to do this for you. The design of your book could spell the difference between success and failure. People quickly spot a poor-quality book.

✔ Edit and proofread. I've already mentioned this, but it cannot be emphasized enough. If you do not have one, buy a book on grammar. I suggest <u>The Elements of Style</u> by William Strunk, Jr. Treat it like your bible for writing. Hire an editor and a proofreader if you possibly can. It is money very well spent. Take some of the responsibility yourself and then work with an expert.

Now you have to sell your book. That will require you to:

✔ Develop a marketing plan. Send advance review copies to book reviewers.

✔ Establish a relationship with a distributor.

✔ Prepare your promotional materials. You will need a media kit, business cards and promotional items such as sell sheets, brochures, bookmarks or postcards.

We have given you a very brief idea of the work involved in running your own publishing company. It can be very rewarding, but it is a tremendous amount of work. You are making a major commitment of time, resources and energy. Many people have achieved success this way. You can too. It is a matter of commitment, education, networking and marketing -- and it is a long-term project.

If, at this point, you're still enthused, then go for it. We wish you success and hope that you will let us know about your company and your books.

Resources for Self-Publishing and Marketing:

(a small selection of books available)

- ✔ Johnson, Robert B. and Pramschufer, Ron. <u>Publishing Basics</u>. Available free as an e-book or soft-cover edition from www.booksjustbooks.com – soft-cover, you pay postage.

- ✔ Howard-Johnson, Carolyn. <u>The Frugal Book Promoter: How to Do What Your Publisher Won't</u>.

- ✔ Hupalo, Peter. <u>How to Start and Run a Small Book Publishing Company: A Small Business Guide to Self-Publishing and Independent Publishing</u>.

- ✔ Jud, Brian. <u>Beyond the Bookstore: How to Sell More Books Profitably to Non-Bookstore Markets</u>.

- ✔ Kremer, John. <u>1001 Ways to Market Your Book</u>.

- ✔ Poynter, Dan. <u>The Self-Publishing Manual: How to Write, Print and Sell Your Own Book</u>.

- ✔ Ross, Marilyn. <u>Jump Start Your Book Sales: A Money-Making Guide for Authors, Independent Publishers and Small Presses</u>.

- ✔ Ross, Tom and Ross, Marilyn. <u>The Complete Guide to Self-Publishing: Everything You Need to Know to Write, Publish, Promote and Sell Your Own Book</u>.

- ✔ Strunk, William, Jr. <u>The Elements of Style</u>.

Scamming the Scammers: Beware Your Own Culpability in Traps and Scams Aimed at Writers

by Joyce Faulkner

Many aspiring scribes dream of scaling to the top of literature's grand pyramid. There they will rub shoulders with the likes of F. Scott Fitzgerald, Harper Lee and J.D. Salinger. Others fantasize about a runaway bestseller and reigning as the next Stephen King.

But for most, fortune is an elusive pixie dancing just beyond their fingertips. Not everyone with a story has the pith, or the vinegar, to finish a book. Not all who do end up with a professional, commercially viable product.

For the gifted, determined few who complete writing projects, the industry is a maze of questionable opportunities, U-turns and dead-ends. The odds against any one writer being at the right place and time with the right book are gargantuan. No wonder many would-be authors end up frustrated, vulnerable and broke.

Impatient with the seemingly endless process, hopeful writers sometimes pay to see their work in print only to feel cheated and embarrassed by the results. It happens so often that everywhere you look there are warnings about fraudulent agents and publishers.

They're useful. Stay clear of anthologies that ask accepted authors to buy several copies. Don't pay reading fees. Be careful of publisher referrals to editors who expect payment. Don't write for free. The laundry list is long.

Certainly, there are scam artists out there who take advantage of those who dream of being "published." Swindlers rely on their victims to participate in the double-cross which makes the result all the more humiliating. However, not all unhappy endings come from fraud. Some new author grief has to do, simply, with unmet expectations.

One writer thinks that once his book is accepted all he has to do is sit back and wait for the royalties to come rolling in. He learns

172

otherwise when his handsome, well-written novel sells a donut hole-full of copies.

Another author pays $500 to a publicist who tells her he'll present her book to the chain bookstore buyers. She imagines dozens of books on the front table at Barnes and Noble. Doesn't happen. There are no guarantees, she quickly learns. Neither of these writers are dupes. They just don't understand the book business and their decisions are injudicious.

Regardless of which publishing approach an author pursues, here are a few attitudinal perspectives that might make the process less stressful.

- ✔ Adjust your expectations. Understand why you are writing and set goals based on that understanding.

- ✔ Evaluate your work with an eye to who might be interested in reading it. Creativity is a wonderful thing, but if you aren't speaking to an audience there will be no one to buy your book. As elementary as that sounds a garage full of unsold books speaks volumes.

- ✔ Understand that regardless of how you publish your book, that's only one part of the process. You must dedicate yourself to selling it. Don't expect anyone else to do this for you, although larger publishers have more resources to help you than do smaller ones.

- ✔ Focus on the art of self-promotion. People won't buy your book if they don't know who you are. There are many books to help with this. One of the best is <u>The Frugal Book Promoter</u> by Carolyn Howard-Johnson.

- ✔ Network with other writers and learn from their successes and mistakes.

- ✔ Have a plan and make tactical decisions that support your strategy. For example, if your goal is to make money from freelance work, don't give away articles. However, if your goal is to create an audience for your books, writing in exchange for advertisement space may be a smart move.

✔ Understand what services you are buying. For example, are you buying results or time? Are you paying for expertise or for a task?

✔ Understand how you are paying for services. Are you paying by the hour? By the project?

✔ If someone with a deal that sounds too good to be true approaches you, it probably is. It's a cliché, but it's true.

Most of us have been disappointed by what we perceive as broken promises. When this is the result of fraud, call a lawyer and take action. Warn others. When it's the result of misunderstanding, making decisions based on inadequate information or choosing the wrong service, there are fewer legal or moral recourses.

Above all, assess why the results were less than you expected. Experience is a great teacher. Too bad it's also a painful one.

first published at *Inkwell Newswatch* (www.fwointl.com/in.html)

Now that you have finished
The Complete Writer

which has guided you through to the publication of your work, you are ready for the next all-important step, promotion. So, you need to obtain The Frugal Book Promoter as a guide to the marketing process.

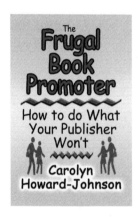

The Frugal Book Promoter
by Carolyn Howard-Johnson
ISBN: 978-1-932993-10-X $17.95

This work offers practical advice the author has gleaned from personal experience. Unlike other books and articles on the subject, this one is detailed – and it's chock full of ideas that even seasoned book promoters will not have tried.

This book is available from your local bookstore, on line supplier or Red Engine Press (www.redenginepress.com).

Want more copies of

The Complete Writer

Just e-mail publisher@redenginepress.com or

fill out the form (or facsimile thereof) and send to:

Red Engine Press

P. O. Box 264

Bridgeville, PA 15017-0264

Name	
Address	
City/State/ZIP	
Number of Copies @ $17.95	
Subtotal	
Sales Tax (PA residence only)	
Postage @ $2.00 1st book, $0.40 additional	
Total Enclosed	

More Great Books from Red Engine Press

Losing Patience
by Joyce Faulkner
ISBN: 978-0-9745652-4-5 $15.95

A good short story sucks you in quickly. Joyce Faulkner creates worlds that absorb you and make you question preconceived notions. Her tales remind one of classic episodes of the *Twilight Zone.*

They Came Home: Korean War POWs Tell Their Stories
by Pat McGrath Avery
ISBN: 978-0-9743758-6-1 $14.95

A must read for Americans to understand the price of freedom and the people who paid that price. This book tells the true stories of three soldiers who were first listed as missing in action and then as prisoners of war in Korea.

In the Shadow of Suribachi   **(COMING IN 2005)**
by Joyce Faulkner
ISBN: 978-0-9745652-0-2 $15.95

Emil Kroner survived the Labor Day hurricane of 1935, Bill Zimmer lost a brother in 1937, Arty Lieberman's relatives were victims of Hitler's fury, Danny Kline lived through the Cleveland Circus fire in 1942, Smitty fell in love with the wrong woman, Cordell was the lucky one, Kirby learned to live with the pain of war. Strangers until they became Marines and their lives changed forever during the battle of Iwo Jima.

Available from Red Engine Press (www.redenginepress.com)

Have Poem Will Travel
by S. Dale "Sierra" Seawright
ISBN: 978-0-9745652-3-7 $9.95

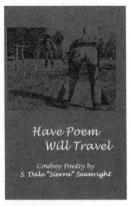

This work from an Oklahoma poet and reenactor, is -- hilarious in places, touching in others. Seawright's talent is natural and raw, reminiscent of the rhythms of Loretta Lynn, Woody Guthrie and Pete Seeger. Seawright performs his poems at nineteenth century western reenactments in Oklahoma, at poetry readings and other state and local events.

One Blue Star
by Mindy Phillips Lawrence
ISBN: 978-0-9745652-5-3 $9.95

This work is a window into the heart of a mother terrified for her children, in love with her country, at odds with her government and no longer willing to take anything at face value. Deeply patriotic and moral, this book of verse explores the lunacy and sorrow of war from the point of view of a parent waiting for her boy to come home.

The Aged Tree Stands Proud
by Pat McGrath Avery
ISBN: 978-0-9663276-1-6 $10.95

No one can live through a crisis and remain unchanged. Pat McGrath Avery's collection of poems recounting her ongoing emotional journey helps us understand that emotional response is a natural part of life.

Available from Red Engine Press (www.redenginepress.com)

Caribbean Calling   (COMING IN 2005)
by J. D. Gordon
ISBN: 978-0-9745652-1-0 $14.95

This story plays out amid lush tropical settings and authentic slices of life in the Florida Keys and Bahamas. It's adventure, action and romance unfolding in an area of the world that is a natural breeding ground for dark characters that deal in everything from gunrunning to drugs and white slavery. It's the resurfacing of old enemies who still carry a grudge. It's the **Caribbean Calling**.

Children's Titles from Red Engine Press

Miller the Green Caterpillar
by Darrell House   Illustrated by Patti Argoff
ISBN: 978-0-9663276-9-1 $16.95

Miller the Green Caterpillar is a children's story told in verse. It's a tale of determination, vision and the belief that sometimes wishes do come true. Darrell is a well-known singer and songwriter from Ft. Lauderdale, Florida. Patti is an accomplished illustrator with several books to her credit. The book is in hardcover. Ages 3 - 8

Underneath the Cushions On The Couch
by Darrell House $15.95

This CD of children's songs appeal to the kid in all of us. The rollicking title song makes us laugh at the obvious.

Available from Red Engine Press (www.redenginepress.com)

The Path Winds Home
by Janie DeVos   Illustrated by Nancy Marsh
ISBN: 978-0-9743758-0-2 $16.95

Sometimes our differences make us stand out in the most positive light. That's the lesson our three little friends, the rabbit, skunk and bear, learn in this delightful new children's story. A must read for a child in today's diversified and multicultural society. The book is in hardcover. Ages 2 - 8

How High Can You Fly?
by Janie DeVos   Illustrated by Renee Rejent
ISBN: 978-0-9663276-2-4 $16.95

A little bird asks his friends if they can fly. He discovers that "All of these creatures on God's precious Earth / Were given a gift of their own at their birth." A story about self-esteem and acceptance of others. The rhyming text appeals to young listeners and readers. The vibrant and expressive illustrations delight children and adults. The book is in hardcover. Ages 2 - 8

Tommy's War
by Pat McGrath Avery   Illustrated by Eric Ray
ISBN: 978-0-9663276-8-3 $5.95

The first in the Kids' World Series, helping kids understand and cope with changes in their lives. Tommy and his friend each have a parent that leaves home because of a war. The story involves family, school and patriotism. 5x7 paperback. Ages 4 - 7

Available from Red Engine Press (www.redenginepress.com)

About the Authors

Beverly Walton-Porter is a Colorado-based professional freelance writer whose work has been featured in numerous publications. She publishes *Scribe & Quill*, an on line newsletter for writers and teaches courses in freelancing and marketing/PR for writers. Her first book, <u>Sun Signs for Writers</u>, will be released by F & W Publications in August 2006.

Mindy Phillips Lawrence is a freelance writer and publicist based in the St. Louis area. Her credits include articles in *Writer's Digest* magazine and *Scribe & Quill* as well as book reviews and interviews for *TheCelebrityCafe.com*, *Scribe & Quill* and *Inkwell Newswatch*. Mindy is the author of <u>One Blue Star,</u> poems about the Military, Families, War and Peace, published by Red Engine Press in October 2004.

Pat McGrath Avery divides her time between south Texas and southwestern Missouri. For the past 15 years, she has been a freelance and contract business writer. She writes nonfiction books as well as reviews and articles for several on line publications. Her most recent book is <u>They Came Home: Korean War POWs Tell Their Stories</u>. She is currently working on another book about veterans. Her first children's book, <u>The Skateboard Zoo,</u> will be out in 2006.

Joyce Faulkner is a Pittsburgh-based author and freelance writer. Her credits include *The Writer*, *Women's Independent Press*, *Byline*, *Scribe & Quill*, *Inkwell Newswatch* and many others. She is a columnist for *TheCelebrityCafe.com*. Her first book was a collection of short fiction titled, <u>Losing Patience</u>. Her next book is scheduled for release from Red Engine Press in 2005. <u>In the Shadow of Suribachi</u> explores the lives of those who fought the Battle of Iwo Jima.